Coll

Student Support Materials for
OCR A2 Sociology

Unit G673
Sociology of Crime and Deviance

D1396357

Authors: Steve Chapman and Fionnuala Swann
Series editor: Peter Langley

Published by Collins Education
An imprint of HarperCollins Publishers
77-85 Fulham Palace Road
Hammersmith
London
W6 8JB

Browse the complete Collins Education catalogue at
www.collinseducation.com

10 9 8 7 6 5 4 3 2 1

ISBN 978-0-00-741837-4

Steve Chapman and Fionnuala Swann assert their moral rights to be identified as the authors of this work.

British Library Cataloguing in Publication Data.

A catalogue record for this publication is available from the British Library.

Commissioned by Charlie Evans and Andrew Campbell

Project editors: Sarah Vittachi and Gudrun Kaiser

Design and typesetting by Hedgehog Publishing Limited

Cover Design by Angela English

Production by Simon Moore

Printed and bound by L.E.G.O. S.p.A. Italy

Indexed by Indexing Specialists (UK) Ltd and Gudrun Kaiser

Acknowledgements

Every effort has been made to contact the holders of copyright material, but if any have been inadvertently overlooked the publishers will be pleased to make the necessary arrangements at the first opportunity.

p12, table 3/ p14/ p34–5 source: Home Office Crime Statistics; p13, table 4, table 5, source: British Crime Survey 2009, ONS; p13/ p44, source: British Crime Survey 2009, ONS; p14, fig 1/ p15, table 6/ p15, fig 2/ p44, source: British Crime Survey 2008, ONS; p31, source: Demos, 2000, www.demos.co.uk; p31, study, source: Michele J. Burman, Susan A. Batchelor and Jane A. Brown, Researching Girls and Violence: Facing the Dilemmas of Fieldwork, *British Journal of Criminology* (2001) 41 (3), 443–459, Oxford University Press; p54, source: HM Prison Service.

Thanks to the following students for providing answers to the questions:

Ruby Barwood, Collette Blackman, Lauren Foley, Vicki Gill, Jessica Gowers, Fran Guratsky, Rachel Hewitt, Ella Keating, Charlotte Ross, Eric Wedge-Bull.

Contents

Defining crime and deviance

Crime is behaviour that breaks the law. **Juvenile delinquency** refers to acts committed by young people, which are criminal or considered anti-social.

To a large extent, it is agreed that all crime is deviant but not all **deviance** is crime. In general, deviance refers to behaviour that most people see as differing from acceptable social norms or standards of society – as abnormal or immoral. Society will often find it impossible to tolerate such behaviour and will thus employ agencies of **social control** to control, suppress or punish such behaviour.

The functionalist definition of crime and deviance

In society, what counts as normality and what counts as deviance is the result of shared values and ways of behaving, or norms. An important aspect of the functionalist theory of crime and deviance is that the deviant is someone who breaks these shared values. Émile Durkheim believed that society was essentially consensual and that most people conform, or aspire to similar values and ways of behaving. Durkheim suggests that every society shares a set of core values, which he called **value consensus** or **collective conscience**. The more behaviour differs from the core values, the more likely it is to be interpreted as deviant. Functionalists argue that social controls exist – **formal social controls** such as laws, and **informal social controls** or norms such as table manners and politeness. In most social situations, these controls clearly identify what is deviant behaviour.

Interactionist definition of crime and deviance

Interactionist sociologists are critical of the functionalist definition of deviance, as it implies that such definitions are fixed, absolute and universally shared. They argue that definitions of normality and deviance are a **social construction**. This means that the same thing, or act, can be interpreted in different ways. Deviance is therefore relative and will depend on factors such as a person's individual point of view, place of living and time-period, culture and the social context in which the activity occurs.

The interactionist approach rejects the idea that modern societies are organized around a **consensus** of values and norms. Instead, interactionists point out that societies are too complex to have a shared set of values. They point out that modern societies are characterized by conflicts of interest and a diversity of beliefs. This approach to deviance suggests that there are competing sets of values, which co-exist. For example, British society includes a range of ethnic minority and religious **subcultures**, and, compared to mainstream white culture, each believes in very different values and therefore definitions of normality and deviance. These values and definitions rarely clash.

Interactionists believe that values, and therefore definitions of normality and deviance, are in a constant state of change as social attitudes evolve over time. Consequently, what counts as normality and deviance, rather than being absolute and fixed, is dynamic and constantly subject to change. However, **interactionism** does acknowledge that some social groups have the power to impose their definitions on others and label them as deviant and criminal.

Conflict theories and definitions of crime and deviance

Conflict theories such as Marxism argue that a consensus of values and norms is unlikely to exist. Marxists believe that modern Western societies are capitalist societies, characterized by extreme inequalities in wealth and power. They argue that the wealthy and powerful **bourgeoisie** – the ruling class – can impose its definitions of normality and deviance on less powerful groups such as the working class and the poor, who are perceived as potential threats to their position. Marxists argue that the law functions to protect ruling-class interests and to criminalize the working class in order to justify control through policing.

Max Weber agreed with Marxism in that the wealthy were able to dominate definitions of what counts as normality and deviance. However, Weber was critical of the fact that Marxists reduced all power and inequality to the economic relationship that existed between the bourgeoisie and **proletariat**. He believed that there were other sources of power and inequality in addition to social class such as race, ethnicity, religion, gender, age, **authority** and **coercion**. For example, feminists argue that in **patriarchal** societies, males define what is normal, and therefore define deviant female behaviour.

Evaluating the social construction of crime

- Some interactionists argue that there is no such thing as 'normal' or 'deviant' behaviour – it is subject to a range of interpretations. But morally, some activities such as rape, child abuse and genocide will never be interpreted positively – they are always wrong.
- This approach suggests that crime and deviance are invented by people with power and are only labels – and are therefore unreal. This is no comfort for victims of crime.
- Interactionists believe that the crime rate can be lowered through **decriminalization**. However, this idea can be applied more easily to trivial rather than serious crimes.

Examiners' notes

Make use of evaluative indicators such as 'however', 'on the other hand' and 'in contrast'.

Essential notes

An example of the Marxist position is the way employers are treated if, for example, their negligence causes a worker's death – the employers are charged with breaches of health and safety rather than manslaughter or murder, thus avoiding a criminal record. If they were prosecuted, the employers would be more likely to be fined than sent to prison.

Essential notes

In **apartheid** South Africa in the 1960s and 1970s, black people were forbidden to use public amenities such as swimming pools or parks because they were reserved for the use of the ruling white minority.

Examiners' notes

Evaluation skills are more important at A2 level than at AS level, so you need to be able to identify specific evaluative points of studies and theories, or contrast theories.

Measuring crime

There are essentially two ways in which sociologists measure crime:

1. They analyse **secondary data** on crime gathered by the government, which could include the official crime statistics (OCS), which are published quarterly and include crimes recorded by the police, and data from the government-sponsored **victim (or victimization) survey** – the **British Crime Survey (BCS)**.
2. They collect **primary data** by conducting victim surveys such as the Islington Crime Survey (ICS) carried out by the **Left Realists**, John Lea and Jock Young, or they might conduct **self-report studies**.

Official crime statistics

The official crime statistics (OCS) have certain strengths and weaknesses:

OCS – strengths	OCS – weaknesses
Very easy and cheap to access – involve little effort on behalf of the sociologist	May not present a complete picture (e.g. the government does not collect statistics relating to the socio-economic background or employment status of people arrested, prosecuted or convicted and sent to prison)
Usually, extremely contemporary (e.g. the 2009 OCS were published in 2010)	Open to political abuse (e.g. crime statistics might be manipulated or 'massaged' by governments for political advantage)
Usually collected in a standardized, systematic and scientific way	Socially constructed (i.e. they are the end result of the decision to record a certain set of activities, so statistics must be collected) – this is the most important weakness (see pp 8–11)
Can be easily checked and verified, so are regarded as highly reliable	Tell us little about the human stories or interpretations that underpin them (e.g. crime and prison statistics reveal little about why people commit crime or what it feels like to be sent to prison)
Allow us to make comparisons between groups (e.g. the OCS cover the whole UK population, which makes it easy to compare things like different groups or regions)	May be based on operational definitions that sociologists would not agree with (e.g. the government may have changed definitions of serious drug offences)
Trends over a period of time can also be easily seen (e.g. sociologists might see less crime as people get older)	
Few ethical problems, as there is no contact with people	
Sociologist does not put him- or herself in any danger	

Table 1
Strengths and weaknesses of official crime statistics

Essential notes

The OCS are our main source of information about crime. Some sociologists accept them uncritically; for example, functionalist and subculturalist sociologists attempt to explain why the working class and young people are more criminal just because the statistics say they are.

Essential notes

The police may engage in administrative practices which result in statistics that are partial in their picture of crime. An example is 'cuffing', which means the police do not record crimes they think they cannot solve, or they may categorize the crimes as 'less important'.

Essential notes

The counting rules used by the police to categorize crimes often change. This makes comparisons between particular time periods very difficult.

Victim (or victimization) surveys

The BCS collects data using structured interviews. See pages 44–45 for the merits of this procedure. Left Realist and feminist victim surveys tend to use unstructured interviews to gather their data and investigate how people feel about being victims of crime.

Unstructured interviews have various strengths and weaknesses:

Unstructured interviews – strengths	Unstructured interviews – weaknesses
Focus on what the victim says or thinks as being the central issue	Said to be unreliable, as they cannot be replicated (repeated) and verified by another sociologist
Allow the researcher to develop trust and **rapport**, thus enabling him or her to view the world through the eyes of the victim	Data difficult to analyse and categorize because of the sheer volume of material in the respondent's own words
Allow the interviewer to make sure that he or she shares the same meaning as the victim, which increases **validity**	Exceptionally time-consuming to conduct and transcribe
Provide richer, more vivid and more **qualitative data** about the experience of being a victim	Expensive to run because training needs to be especially thorough and specialized

Examiners' notes

The merits of unstructured interviews can be used to evaluate the methodology used in the BCS.

Table 2
Strengths and weaknesses of unstructured interviews

Self-report studies

A self-report is a type of questionnaire, which attempts to uncover the true amount of crime in society. It lists a number of petty criminal acts and asks respondents to tick those they have successfully committed without being caught. To improve validity, the questionnaires stress confidentiality and anonymity for the respondent.

Ian Marsh notes that validity is undermined by under-reporting and over-reporting. People may under-report because self-report studies are retrospective and depend on respondents remembering crimes committed 12 months before. Some people exaggerate offences to create a 'tough' impression. Others keep quiet, fearing that the police will be informed.

The representativeness of self-report questionnaires is questioned for three reasons:

1. It is impossible to include all criminal acts in a questionnaire. This means the researcher must be selective, which raises problems as to which offences to include or not.
2. Self reports are distributed mainly to young people – it would be difficult to get businessmen to cooperate and admit to **white-collar crime** or **corporate crime**.
3. Josine Junger-Tas (1989) reports a sliding scale of responses to self-report questionnaires, depending on how much contact respondents have had with the criminal justice system. Response rates from individuals with a criminal record were lower than from those without.

Examiners' notes

The methods used to collect information about crime have distinct strengths and weaknesses, so make sure you assess them as part of your evaluative approach to how crime and deviance are socially constructed, or to victimization.

- -

Essential notes

The counting rules that all police forces in the UK have to use to categorize and count crimes are constantly changing, which makes it difficult to compare crimes today with 'similar' crimes in the past. Moreover, the government contributes to this difficulty by continually introducing new laws, and therefore new crimes.

Essential notes

An example of not wanting to involve the police is when a school expels or suspends students for criminal activity such as vandalism and drugs, rather than involve the police – so these crimes will not be part of the OCS.

Essential notes

The dark figure of crime is an important idea, which you should be able to describe in detail. Its existence was particularly highlighted by the BCS when it was found that respondents reported crimes to survey researchers, but not to the police. Recent BCS survey data suggests that the dark figure may be receding because the gap between crimes reported to the police and crimes reported to the BCS is at its narrowest since the BCS began.

Social construction of the official crime statistics

It is often assumed, particularly by the mass media, that the official crime statistics (OCS) are reliable and valid in the picture of crime and criminality that they present. However, **interpretivist sociologists** argue that the OCS are of limited usefulness and are in fact a social construction. They tell us more about the social groups involved in their collection – the general public, victims, the mass media, the police and the courts – than they tell us about crime and criminals.

Interpretivists point out that the OCS do not account for all the crime committed in the UK. They account only for those crimes that are recognized as such by victims and by the police. Sociologists have long argued that there exists a **dark figure** (sometimes referred to as the hidden iceberg) of unrecorded crime. It may be that the social characteristics of those who are not reported or caught may differ from those who are.

The existence of this dark figure of crime can be illustrated in various ways:

- Some criminal offences are not included in the OCS, such as tax and VAT fraud or health and safety infringements. These offences are more likely to be committed by individuals who are wealthy and powerful.
- The police may exercise discretion in terms of how they define and then count crime because of political pressures to improve their clear-up rates or to improve efficiency. For example, the police often engage in a practice called **coughing**, in which they persuade criminals to admit to crimes they may not have committed. This is of benefit to the police because the crimes are 'cleared-up', and to the criminal because the courts tend to pass sentence more leniently to defendants who admit guilt. However, it means that the OCS may not be an authentic picture of crime.
- Some offenders may belong to institutions such as the armed services, which police and punish criminals outside of the legal system. Public and state schools, professional associations such as the British Medical Association (BMA) and the Law Society, and financial institutions such as banks, prefer not to involve the police and courts because of the bad publicity that may be generated for their institutions.
- There is also evidence from the British Crime Survey (BCS) that many people, especially ethnic minorities, do not report crime because they have little faith in the police.
- Some victims may not be aware that a crime has been committed against them. An example is child abuse, which provides inaccurate statistics for exactly this reason.
- Some victims may fear humiliation at the hands of the police, the courts, the media and society in general, and so will be reluctant to report crime against them to the authorities. Rape, in particular, is thought to be greatly under-estimated by the OCS because of this.

The general public and victims of crime

Andy Pilkington argues that the OCS may not be useful because these statistics only tell us about the increased reporting of particular crimes by the general public and victims of crime, rather than actual increases in crime itself. For example:

- The general public has grown more intolerant of property crime as people have become more prosperous and **materialistic**. This has led to a greater public willingness to report theft and burglary. Increased affluence has also led to more people taking out insurance, which encourages reporting of property crime and criminal damage by victims.

- The OCS for some juvenile crimes may simply reflect public intolerance, fuelled by journalists' construction of **moral panics** in search of newsworthy stories – those guaranteed to sell newspapers or attract large television audiences. Moral panics increase the profile of the **folk devils** – groups regarded as a bad influence on society – so that the general public is more likely to recognize the problem and report it. This puts the police under pressure to curb the problem, which may lead to more arrests and prosecutions. The government may pass new laws in order to control the so-called problem. The folk devil group may react by becoming more confrontational and criminal. In other words, the moral panic leads to **deviancy amplification** – an artificial rise in crime statistics (see p 48).

- Some crimes such as soft drug offences and prostitution appear to have no victim, and therefore may not be reported by the general public as consistently as other crimes. These **victimless crimes** depend on police detection. Such detection varies from area to area. Some police forces may ignore prostitution or soft drug use, whereas others may frequently crack down on these offences. As a result, it is often difficult for sociologists to trust or compare the statistics relating to these crimes.

When taking these factors into consideration, criminologists have estimated that for every 100 crimes committed, 47 will be reported to the police, 27 will be recorded by the police, and five will be cleared up in the form of a caution or conviction. Self-report studies indicate that the volume of crime should be greater and that females and middle-class males are just as likely to commit a crime as those included in the crime statistics.

Examiners' notes

The skill of knowledge and understanding refers to whether you are demonstrating the ability to outline and describe the debate using the appropriate theories and studies. For example, the debate about crime statistics is usually organized into four theoretical approaches: **positivist**, interpretivist (or interactionist), Marxist and Left Realist.

■☞ This topic continues on the next pages

The police

Interpretivists argue that the OCS tell us more about the nature of policing in the UK than about crime and criminality. In particular, they may tell us a great deal about how police officers interact with suspects, especially those from relatively powerless social groups. Therefore, interpretivists question the validity of the picture of criminality that the OCS provide. They suggest that young, working-class and African-Caribbean people frequently appear in these statistics because they are profiled and targeted by the police rather than because they are more criminal. This can be illustrated in several ways:

- Studies of police officers on patrol conducted by Joan Smith, Christopher Grey and Aaron Cicourel indicate that they operate using stereotypical assumptions or labels about what constitutes 'suspicious' or 'criminal' behaviour; that is, the decision to stop or arrest someone may be based on whether they correspond to a **stereotype**.

- There is strong evidence from Simon Holdaway, Ben Bowling, Coretta Phillips and the MacPherson Report that suggests racial profiling by some police officers may be a crucial element governing their decision to stop African-Caribbeans. Statistics released in 2010 show that police **stop and search** African-Caribbeans six times more often and Asians twice as often as white people. Sociological studies of the occupational or **canteen culture** of the police suggest that it sustains racist attitudes among some rank and file police officers. Holdaway found that older and more experienced officers use racist language as a matter of course in the presence of younger officers, while Bowling and Phillips noted that some police officers in London based their decision to stop young black males in cars on a stereotype known as 'driving while black'. Police officers assumed that black youths were driving upmarket cars because either they were drug dealers or they had stolen them. John Lea and Jock Young also note a military-style police presence in ethnic-minority dominated areas, which may result in more confrontation between police and young black people, which artificially amplifies the OCS.

- Holdaway notes that, in general, young people – particularly those from working-class backgrounds – are more likely to fit police stereotypes about criminality than older or middle-class people. These stereotypes are likely to lead to a greater police presence in some urban neighbourhoods.

- Feminist criminologists argue that male officers tend to adopt **paternalistic** attitudes towards female offenders, who are less likely to be stopped, arrested and charged. For example, when caught committing criminal offences, they are more likely to be cautioned than arrested and charged. Pollack calls this the **chivalry factor**. According to Ministry of Justice statistics in 2007, 49% of female offenders received a caution. Only 30% of male offenders received the same. Research also indicates that police culture is very masculine (fewer than 20% of police officers are women) and interaction with men or ethnic minorities may be shaped by a need to be seen by other officers as being tough.

The courts

There is evidence that juries and judges also engage in stereotyping. It has been found that middle-class offenders and women are much more likely to be found not guilty by juries. When they are found guilty, they are treated more leniently by an upper-class male-dominated judiciary. Roger Hood's observations of criminal courts found that even when black youths were up for the same offence as white youths, they were 17% more likely to get a prison sentence. The OCS may therefore tell us more about judicial attitudes than about crime and criminality.

Marxist critique of the OCS

Marxists are also very critical of the OCS. They suggest that the capitalist state collects and constructs crime statistics in order to serve the interests of the ruling class. The statistics serve an **ideological function** – whoever has the power to collect and construct such statistics has the power to control and manipulate public opinion. Therefore Marxists argue that the ideological function of the OCS is to criminalize groups such as the young, the working class and African-Caribbeans. This divides and rules the working class by diverting white conformist working-class attention away from class inequalities.

Furthermore, Steven Box argues that the OCS divert attention from both middle-class white-collar crime and corporate crime. Box argues that crimes committed by the powerful are not pursued as vigorously or punished as harshly as working-class crimes. He also argues that the powerful engage in anti-social activities, which result in death, injury and theft for ordinary people but are often not defined as criminal because the ruling class constructs laws to reflect their own interests.

However, in contrast, Left Realists such as Jock Young and John Lea (see p 26) note that the Islington Crime Survey (ICS) data suggests that the OCS are largely correct and that young working-class people and, depending on the area, African-Caribbean people do commit more crime than other social groups despite the influence of moral panics, police stereotyping and judicial bias.

Examiners' notes

In addition to demonstrating knowledge and understanding, you will be expected to engage in analysis, evaluation and application (AO2 skills). In particular, this means that you need to use examples to illustrate ideas, concepts and theories, or use statistics to reinforce specific points you are making. Evaluation is crucial – you will need to identify some strengths and weaknesses of particular studies, theories and approaches in order to maximize your marks.

Patterns of crime and deviance

British sociologists get much of their information about patterns and trends in crime from the official crime statistics (OCS). Published quarterly by the government, these are based on:

- crimes reported by victims and the general public, and recorded by the police
- crimes detected and 'cleared up', or solved, by the police
- crimes reported to the British Crime Survey (BCS). The BCS, introduced in 1983, is an annual survey of crime victimization, in which about 47 000 adults aged 16 or over and living in private households in England and Wales are interviewed face-to-face about their experiences as victims of property crimes such as burglary, and personal crimes such as assault.

The BCS is thought to provide a more realistic picture of household and personal crime than the OCS because it includes crimes that are not reported to the police or recorded by them.

The OCS are used to establish trends and patterns in criminal activity, especially to do with:

- the volume of crime – how much of it there is and if it is increasing or decreasing
- the main types of crime – whether or not it takes the form of violence against the person or is property-orientated
- the 'typical' social characteristics of the people who are reported, arrested and convicted.

The OCS are also useful because they can be used to assess the effectiveness of criminal justice initiatives such as the **Anti-Social Behaviour Order (ASBO)** or an increase in the recruitment of police officers. A significant rise or fall in the statistics may indicate the success or failure of a particular **social policy**.

Trends in crime

Robert Reiner suggests that there are three distinct periods, which show the trends in criminal behaviour.

Period 1: late 1950s to early 1980s – rapid rise in recorded crime

During this period, the OCS suggested that there was a dramatic rise in the volume of recorded crime in the UK and that all major categories of crime had substantial increases. (Until 1983 only crimes reported to and recorded by the police were used to measure crime.)

Types of crimes	1971	1984
Violence against the person (e.g. murder)	47 000	114 000
Sexual offences (e.g. rape and child abuse)	23 000	20 000
Burglary	451 000	897 000
Robbery (e.g. armed robbery and mugging)	7 500	25 000
Theft and handling stolen goods (e.g. shoplifting)	1 003 000	1 808 000
Fraud and forgery	99 800	126 000

Table 3
Change in types of crimes from 1971–84

Period 2: 1984 to 1993 – crime explosion

Between 1984 and 1993 the number of crimes recorded by the police increased by 111%. The number of crimes reported in the BCS, used alongside the OCS after 1983, rose by 77% during the same period.

Types of crimes	1984	1993
Violence against the person	114 000	205 000
Property crimes	3 325 000	5 191 000
Vehicle offences	750 000	1 523 000

Table 4
Change in types of crimes between 1984–93

Period 3: 1994 to 2009 – falling crime, rising fear

Between 1994 and 2009 the crime rate fell significantly, in both the crimes recorded by the police and those reported to the BCS.

Types of crimes	1994	2009
Violence against the person	218 000	872 000
Property crimes	4 895 000	3 032 000
Vehicle offences	1 384 000	495 000

Table 5
Change in types of crimes between 1994–2009

Despite the overall fall in crime, recorded violence during the last 25 years has increased as a proportion of all crime. In 1997 violent crime made up only 8% of all crime, but in 2009 violence accounted for 21% of all reported and recorded crime.

However, we need to make four important observations:

1. During 1998–99 the counting rules for crime used by the police changed significantly. In 2002 the National Crime Recording Standard (NCRS) was introduced. These changes resulted in the introduction of new offences, especially for less serious violent crime, and led to a steep rise in violence statistics.
2. The amount of violence reported to the BCS has declined. Since 1995 the number of violent incidents reported to the BCS has halved (50%) and is now at a similar level to that in 1981. This drop represents two million fewer incidents and about 800 000 fewer victims in 2009–10 compared to 1995.
3. Many types of serious violence such as manslaughter, murder, aggravated and grievous bodily harm and the use of guns and knives have actually declined since the 1980s. However, in 2009, serious sexual crime increased by 7% compared to 2008.
4. As a proportion of all crime, violent crime has increased during the past 10 years because property crime has declined steeply since the mid-1990s.

Interpretivist sociologists suggest that the methods used for collecting and socially constructing crime statistics are unreliable, so the picture of crime offered by the OCS does not reflect the reality of crime.

Examiners' notes

It is important to use mass media sources to keep up-to-date with crime trends such as the OCS. Note any interesting patterns and trends to show the examiners that you are aware of contemporary issues.

Examiners' notes

To achieve marks for AO2 skills, use specific examples to show a clear picture of how crime rates have changed over the past 30 years. Also try to be evaluative; for example, new laws are made and counting rules are changed, so it is not possible to compare crime in 2011 with crime in 1981.

Essential notes

A group of crimes committed by young people, collectively known as juvenile delinquency, have been singled out by some sociologists. Generally, these crimes do not involve financial reward, but may be committed because of boredom, a search for thrills, and sometimes, malice. The crimes are usually committed by subcultures or gangs and include joy-riding, tagging, anti-social behaviour such as harassing members of the community, hooliganism, vandalism, territorial gang violence and drug-taking.

Social distribution of crime by age, gender, ethnicity, locality and social class

An examination of statistics relating to police stops and arrests, convictions in the courts and the prison population suggests that some social groups tend to be more criminal than others.

Age

About 50% of all crimes are committed by young people. Statistical evidence shows that the older a person is, the less likely he or she is to commit a crime. Most burglary, street robbery, violence against the person, shoplifting and criminal damage is committed by young people aged 17–24. The peak age for known male offenders is 18, compared to 15 for females.

Gender

About 80% to 90% of offenders found guilty or cautioned are male. As a result, male crime is said to outnumber female crime by an approximate ratio of 5 to 1. At least one-third of men are likely to be convicted for a criminal offence, compared to only 8% of women.

It has been found that men and women are convicted for different types of offences. For example, males dominate all offences but female conviction is likely to be for theft, particularly shoplifting. However, in recent years there has been a rapid rise in violence committed by young women (although it is still vastly outnumbered by male violent offences).

This graph shows the relationships between age, gender and crime.

Fig 1
Offenders as a percentage of the population: by age, 2006, England and Wales

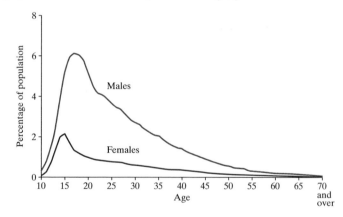

Essential notes

It is important to understand that most theories of crime are aimed at explaining male criminality. Some feminist sociologists argue that this 'malestream' criminology reflects patriarchal inequality. However, it also reflects the reality that in 2008 there were 4474 women in prison out of a total prison population of more than 83 000 – a mere 5.4%.

Ethnicity

Prison statistics show an over-representation of African-Caribbean men and women in prison – about one-tenth of male prisoners and one-fifth of female prisoners in UK prisons are African-Caribbean – yet this ethnic minority group makes up only 2.2% of the population. The police stop and search more black people than other groups and black youths are more likely to be cautioned or given an ASBO than any other ethnic minority group. There has been a rise in the number of Asians who are arrested and convicted but their numbers are still below the national average.

This table summarizes some of the patterns in the relationship between ethnicity and crime.

	Ethnicity						Total
	White	Mixed	Black	Asian	Chinese or Other	Not stated/ Unknown	
General population aged 10 & over (2001 census)	91.3	1.3	2.2	4.4	0.9	0.0	100
Stops and searches[1]	68.1	2.5	13.1	8.1	1.2	7.0	100
Arrests[2]	79.3	2.8	7.4	5.1	1.4	4.0	100
Cautions[2][3]	82.5		6.5	4.6	1.4	5.0	100
Youth offences	84.8	3.5	5.8	3.0	0.4	2.5	100
Tried at Crown Court[3][4]	73.5		14.0	8.0	4.4		100
Court ordered supervision by probation service[5]	83.6	2.5	6.3	4.6	1.2	1.8	100
Prison receptions[6]	79.1	2.9	10.6	5.9	1.2	0.2	100

Table 6
Percentage of ethnic groups at different stages of the criminal justice process compared to the ethnic breakdown of the general population, England and Wales 2007–08
Note:
Figures may not add up to 100% due to rounding.

[1] Stop and searches recorded by the police under section 1 of the Police and Criminal Evidence Act 1984 and other legislation.
[2] Notifiable offences.
[3] The data in these rows is based on ethnic appearance, and as such does not include the category Mixed ethnicity (the data in the rest of the table is based on self-identified ethnicity).
[4] Information on ethnicity is missing in 19% of cases; therefore, percentages are based on known ethnicity.
[5] Commencements.
[6] Sentenced.

Locality

Urban areas, especially inner-city areas and council estates, have higher rates of crime than suburbs or rural areas. (Refer to the bar chart.) The inner-city and council estate residents (the urban poor), especially the elderly, are more likely than other social groups to be the victims of crime.

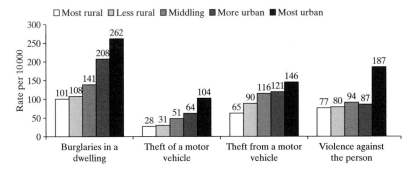

Fig 2
Recorded crime rates per 10 000 population by area type (2000–01)

Social class

Robert Reiner notes that there is a working-class bias in the prison population. Prior to being imprisoned, 74% were either unemployed or employed at the lowest occupational levels. Ann Hagell and Tim Newburn's study of youth detention centres found that only 8% of persistent offenders came from middle-class backgrounds. Offences can also be differentiated by social class. Middle-class offenders tend to be associated with white-collar crime, fraud and tax evasion; working-class offenders are found guilty mainly of burglary and street crime.

Essential notes

Durkheim's theory attempts to explain why most people conform rather than commit crime. It focuses on social control and conformity rather than on why certain groups commit more crime compared to other groups.

Functionalist explanations of crime and deviance

Functionalists argue that crime and deviance can only be explained by looking at the way societies are organized socially – their **social structures** – and that crime is caused by society rather than the circumstances of the individual. Functionalism is therefore a **structuralist theory** of crime.

Émile Durkheim

Émile Durkheim believed that in pre-industrial societies, crime was rare because family and religion were powerful agencies of socialization and social control. This ensured an influential combination of consensus and community, which exercised a powerful influence over personal behaviour. Durkheim also believed that crime rates were higher in industrial cities because the complexity of modern life undermined the **authority** of religion and family. Consensus, community and social controls are weaker, so people are more likely to experience **anomie** – a sense of moral confusion that weakens their commitment to shared values and rules, thus encouraging crime and deviance.

Durkheim observed that crime and deviance were present in all societies. He speculated that crime functions for the benefit of society in various ways:

Examiners' notes

Always try to illustrate points with examples. Examiners like to see candidates applying their knowledge because it indicates understanding (if it is correct).

- Acts of crime and deviance can provoke positive social change by highlighting aspects of the social structure or law that are inadequate. For example, the Suffragette movement broke the law in order to highlight gender inequalities.
- Some crimes such as terrorist attacks create public outrage, which reinforces community solidarity against the offenders.
- Pursuit, trial and punishment of criminals reassures people that society is functioning effectively, while reminding them of acceptable social boundaries of behaviour.
- Some minor crimes are worth tolerating as a safety valve, as they prevent more serious crimes taking place.

Evaluation of Durkheim

- He never explains why certain social groups commit crime.
- He neglects the fact that some crimes are always **dysfunctional**.
- Marxists argue that he underestimates the level of conflict and inequality in modern societies.

Robert Merton

Robert Merton argued that the cause of crime lies in the relationship between the culture and the social structure of society. In capitalist societies, cultural institutions such as the mass media socialize individuals into believing that material success is a realistic goal.

Essential notes

We can apply Merton's theory to most Western capitalist economies, including the UK – considering how its cultural goals are organized around the inter-related values of monetary success, celebrity status, consumerism and materialism.

However, Merton notes that resources and opportunities are not fairly distributed in capitalist societies. Those at the bottom of society may experience a **strain** between their goals and the legitimate institutional means of achievement (education and work), as access to these is blocked by those with economic and social advantages. This can produce anomie, which, Merton argued, individuals could respond to in various ways:

Response	Method of individual's response
Conformity	Most of the population cope with disappointment by continuing to do their best and making the most of what society offers them
Innovation	Commitment to cultural goals may remain strong, but some people reject the conventional means of acquiring wealth and turn to illegal means
Ritualism	Some people have lost sight of material goals, but derive satisfaction from fairly meaningless jobs
Retreatism	A small number of people reject both the goals and the means, by dropping out of society
Rebellion	People may rebel and seek to replace shared goals and institutional means with radical alternatives, and may use violent methods to achieve this

Table 7
Responses to anomie

Merton concludes that criminals are not that different from law-abiding citizens. They have the same goals – to achieve material success.

Evaluation of Merton

- Merton does not explain why some individuals commit crime, yet others conform, retreat or rebel.
- Merton's theory explains crime that results in economic gain, but he does not explain many forms of violent and sexual crimes.
- He also fails to explain crimes committed by young people in gangs, which do not seem to be motivated by material goals.
- White-collar crime and corporate crime arise from access to opportunities rather than the blocking of them.
- Merton fails to ask who benefits from the capitalist system and especially the laws that underpin it. Marxists, like Steven Box, suggest that the ruling capitalist class benefits most from the way laws are currently organized.

However, Sumner claims that Merton has uncovered the main cause of crime in modern societies – the alienation caused by disillusionment with the impossible goals set by **capitalism**.

Examiners' notes

Successful evaluation is balanced evaluation – it should contain reference to the strengths as well as the weaknesses of particular studies or theories.

Essential notes

Be aware of the other theories that Merton influenced, especially Cohen's subcultural theory, and Cloward and Ohlin's theory of illegitimate opportunity structure and Cashmore's theory as to why black youth might commit crime (see pp 18–19, 35).

Key study

Jock Young is a sociologist and criminologist. His work, *The Vertigo of Late Modernity* (2009), is very much influenced by Merton's ideas.

Young argues that key institutions in the UK such as educational establishments and the media stress the **meritocratic** ideal. He also argues that meritocracy is a myth and that a 'chaos of inequality' characterizes financial rewards in the UK – business leaders and celebrities are paid huge sums of money, yet hard-working people in full-time jobs struggle to survive. Young argues that there is a contradiction between culture, which focuses on monetary success and acquiring material goods, and the institutions that make up the social structure, which fail to deliver material success for most people. He notes that this contradiction produces anomie, and much violent criminality is the response.

Examiners' notes

If you are required to answer a question on crime committed by young people or the working class, it can be helpful to begin with an outline of Cohen's ideas.

Subcultural explanations of crime and deviance

Subcultural theory focuses on explaining why young working-class people commit crime. Known as juvenile delinquency, it is often malicious in nature and not linked to gaining material or financial goals. Subcultural theory also tries to explain why juvenile delinquency has a collective or subcultural character – it is committed as part of a larger group or gang.

Albert Cohen

Albert Cohen, like Merton, argues that delinquency is caused by a strain between cultural goals and the institutional means of achieving them. He suggests that young people want status, respect and to feel valued. Middle-class youngsters usually attain these things from their parents, teachers and peers as they achieve educational success.

However, Cohen suggests that working-class boys are denied status at school, as their parents have failed to equip them with the skills they need. Thus, these boys are placed in the bottom sets, and consequently are unable to acquire the knowledge and status enjoyed by students in the higher sets. Such boys may leave school with few or no qualifications and then work in low-paid jobs or are unemployed. In this sense, they are denied status by wider society.

Cohen argues that these experiences result in low self-esteem. These boys feel alienated and angry at the low status that schools and society allocate them. They experience a form of anomie, called '**status frustration**' by Cohen. They respond by forming gangs or subcultures of like-minded boys who reverse the norms and values of the dominant culture and award status on the basis of anti-school and delinquent behaviour.

Essential notes

Despite the fact that Cohen's theory is over 50 years old, most contemporary sociologists investigating gang culture today acknowledge that his idea of status frustration is a central cause of why some young people are attracted to joining gangs.

Evaluation of Cohen

- Paul Willis (see p 38) concludes that the working-class youths in Cohen's study of working-class under achievement did not share the same definition of status as middle-class boys. They defined educational failure as 'success' because qualifications were not necessary for the types of factory jobs they wanted.
- Most working-class boys actually conform at school despite educational failure.
- Cohen ignores female delinquency.
- He neglects the role of the agencies of social control in the social construction of delinquency. For example, police stereotyping of working-class youths might mean they are more likely to be stopped and searched.

Essential notes

Think about the strengths and limitations of this type of research.

Key study

John Pitts studied gangs in Waltham Forest in London. After speaking to social workers, police officers and gang members, he found that 'respect' or status was most the most important goal of gang culture.

The study showed that status was gained by projecting a **hyper-masculine** identity and taking part in territorial conflict. Showing disrespect was regarded as a major type of deviance and often provoked a violent response.

Source: Lansley, S. *Rich Britain,* Politico's Publishing Ltd

Walter Miller

Walter Miller argues that working-class juvenile delinquents are merely acting out and exaggerating the mainstream values of working-class subculture. Miller suggests that working-class youths' subculture has developed a series of **focal concerns**, which give meaning to their lives outside work. These include an increased sense of masculinity – which sees violence as an acceptable problem-solving device – a desire for thrills and being anti-authority. Living out these focal concerns compensates for boredom at school and in factory jobs, but they are also likely to cause confrontation with teachers and the police. Miller therefore blames working-class delinquency on what he sees as the potentially deviant nature of working-class culture.

Richard Cloward and Lloyd Ohlin

Richard Cloward and Lloyd Ohlin argue that the type of crime committed by young people depends on the **illegitimate opportunity structure** available in their area. They identify three types of illegitimate opportunity structures, which produce three types of subcultures:

1. In some areas, there are established patterns of illegitimate opportunity in which people experience criminal careers. These organized types of criminal subcultures mirror legitimate businesses, in that employees have specific roles and can be promoted upwards to managerial or executive status. Sudhir Venkatesh observed such a subculture in Chicago in his study *Gang Leader for a Day*.
2. Some inner-city areas may be dominated by conflict subcultures, which engage in highly masculinized territorial or respect-driven violence. Pitts found that local youth in inner-city London found it difficult to resist gang membership because the risk to themselves and their families from non-affiliation was too great.
3. If young people fail to gain access to either the criminal or conflict subcultures, they may form retreatist subcultures, in which the major activities are drug use and commit crimes such as burglary and shoplifting to finance it.

Criticisms of subcultural theory

David Matza suggests that subcultural theories have the following problems:

- Most young working-class people experience status frustration but do not become delinquents.
- Only a minority of youths actually become delinquents.
- Some young people drift in and out of delinquency, eventually growing out of it when they reach adulthood.
- When justifying or explaining their delinquency, young people rarely refer to membership of subcultures.
- Subcultural theories generally neglect the role of the police, who may target young working-class people as potentially criminal and frequently stop, search and arrest them, whereas they ignore similar behaviour in high-status groups.

Essential notes

It is important to realize that Miller's theory, although a subcultural theory, bears little resemblance to Cohen's theory, which partly blames society for gang activity. Miller strongly implies that working-class culture is problematic and inferior compared to middle-class culture. His theory is not dissimilar to the '**underclass**' theory of Charles Murray.

Essential notes

Most interactionist sociologists, such as Matza, believe that crime and deviance are a social construction – the end product of decisions made by the powerful, who define particular activities as criminal or deviant because they disapprove of them. The frequent appearance of young or working-class people in crime statistics reflects their lack of power. Their behaviour is more likely to be defined as problematic, so they are targeted by the police. Subcultural theories aim to explain why young working-class people commit crime because the official crime statistics (OCS) say they do. Yet, these statistics may not be valid.

Marxist explanations of crime and deviance

Marxists argue that the nature and organization of capitalism creates the potential for criminal behaviour. This can be illustrated in two ways.

1. David Gordon argues that capitalism is characterized by class inequalities in the distribution of, for example, wealth and income, poverty, unemployment and homelessness. He suggests that most working-class crime is a realistic and rational response to these inequalities. Gordon argues that, considering the nature of capitalism, we should not ask 'why the working-class commit crime' but instead 'why they don't commit more crime'.

2. Gordon argues that the **ideology** of capitalism encourages criminal behaviour in all social classes; for example, values such as competition, materialism and consumerism as well as the profit motive encourage a culture of greed and self-interest. The need to win at all costs or go out of business, as well as the desire for self-enrichment, encourages capitalists to commit white-collar and corporate crimes such as tax evasion. Capitalism also encourages a 'culture of envy' among poorer sections of society, which may also encourage a criminal reaction.

The law as ideology and social control

Marxists, such as Louis Althusser, argue that the law is an **ideological state apparatus**, which functions in the interests of the capitalist class to maintain and legitimate class inequality in the following ways:

- It is concerned mainly with protecting the major priorities of capitalism – wealth, private property and profit. Laureen Snider notes that the capitalist state is reluctant to pass laws that regulate the activities of businesses or threaten their profitability.
- Box notes that the powerful kill, injure, maim and steal from ordinary members of society but these killings, injuries and thefts are often not covered by the law. For example, a worker's death due to employer infringements of health and safety laws is a civil, rather than criminal offence.
- Law enforcement is selective and tends to favour the rich and powerful. For example, social security fraud, largely committed by the poor, inevitably attracts prosecution and often prison, yet tax fraudsters, who are usually wealthy and powerful individuals rather than ordinary taxpayers, rarely get taken to court.
- Jeffrey Reiman (2001) argues that the more likely a crime is to be committed by higher-class people, the less likely it is to be treated as a criminal offence. In particular, white-collar and corporate crimes are under-policed and under-punished.

White-collar and corporate crime

Hazel Croall defines white-collar crime as crime committed in the course of legitimate employment, which involves the abuse of an occupational role. Croall suggests fraud, accounting offences, tax evasion, insider dealing and computer crime as being typical white-collar crimes.

Croall notes that people who own the means of production or who manage them have greater opportunities than most to make large sums of money from crime.

Croall notes that companies also commit crimes, known as corporate crimes. Examples are:

Type of crime	Example
Crimes against consumers	Manufacturing and selling dangerous goods or foods; not ensuring the safety of passengers
Crimes against employees	In the UK, between 1965 and 1995, 25 000 people were killed in the workplace; about 70% of these deaths were due to employer violation of health and safety laws
Environmental offences	Pollution
Financial fraud	False accounting; share price fixing

Croall argues that despite the fact that the costs of corporate and white-collar crimes far outstrip the overall combined annual value of burglary, theft and robbery, they are not regarded as a serious problem by the general public for the following reasons:

- These offences are often invisible and hidden from the public gaze. People do not fear white-collar or corporate crime in the same way as they do robbery or violence.
- Many of these crimes are complex, as they involve the abuse of technical, financial or scientific knowledge.
- Responsibility is often delegated or diffused in companies, so it may be difficult to decide where blame lies.
- Victimization tends to be indirect – offenders and victims rarely come face-to-face, and many people may not realize that they have been victims of a crime.
- Croall notes that there is often a very fine line between what are morally acceptable and unacceptable business practices.
- Many of the regulatory bodies, which monitor these types of crimes advise and warn offenders rather than punish them. Corporate offenders are rarely taken to court.

Evaluation of traditional Marxism
- It largely ignores the relationship between crime and important non-class variables such as ethnicity and gender.
- Not all poor people commit crime, despite the pressures of living in poverty in a money-obsessed society.
- The criminal justice system sometimes acts against the interests of the capitalist class.

Essential notes

Marxists argue that capitalism is 'criminogenic' – this means that it is a natural outcome of capitalist practices and values.

Table 8
Examples of corporate crimes

Essential notes

Think about how you would explain why people who are already rich and powerful might be motivated to commit crimes. The ideas of Gordon, functionalists and Left Realists might help.

Examiners' notes

A key evaluative point that you might make with regard to Marxism is that white-collar and corporate crime are difficult to research because of their nature and the fact that perpetrators have the power to deny sociologists access to; for example, their offices, companies and staff.

Neo-Marxist explanations of crime and deviance – the 'New Criminology'

Neo-Marxists are sociologists who have been influenced by many of the ideas of traditional Marxism, which they combine with ideas from other approaches, such as **labelling theory**.

The 'New Criminology' of Ian Taylor, Paul Walton and Jock Young is the most well-known example of Neo-Marxism. This generally agrees with the traditional Marxist analysis that:

- Capitalist society is based on exploitation and class conflict and characterized by extreme inequalities of wealth and power.
- The state makes and enforces laws in the interests of the capitalist class and criminalizes members of the working class.

However, Neo-Marxists are critical of traditional Marxism, which they argue is too deterministic. For example:

Traditional Marxists	See the working class as the passive victims of capitalism, who are driven to criminality by factors beyond their control
Neo-Marxists	Reject the ideas of the traditional Marxists. Instead, they are 'voluntarists', which means they believe that individuals have free will. They argue that the working-class and members of ethnic minority groups experience the constraints of capitalism and then make choices about how they should react to this experience

Table 9
Example of the difference between traditional Marxism and Neo-Marxism

From a Neo-Marxist perspective, crime is a deliberate and meaningful political response by the powerless to their position within the capitalist system. The poor and the powerless commit crime as a way of protesting against injustice, exploitation and alienation. Neo-Marxists claim that crimes against property, such as theft and burglary, are a reaction to wealth inequality. Vandalism is a symbolic attack on society's obsession with property. Criminals are therefore not the passive victims of capitalism – they are actively struggling to alter capitalism and to change society for the better.

Neo-Marxists argue that the ruling class is aware of the revolutionary potential of working-class crime and has taken steps to control it – state apparatuses such as the police target working-class areas, while the state has introduced 'repressive' laws such as the Criminal Justice Acts to control the 'problem' population. Stuart Hall claims that moral panics about potentially disruptive groups such as the young and ethnic minorities are often created by the mass media working on behalf of the state in order to divide and rule a potentially troublesome working class. Hall analysed how the tabloid media presented 'mugging' or street robbery in the 1970s as a new crime in which black criminals robbed white victims. He claims this had the ideological function of dividing the black and white working class and setting them against each other, thereby diverting attention from the mismanagement of capitalism in this period by the ruling class.

Essential notes

The Neo-Marxist theory sees working-class criminals as politically motivated by their negative experience of capitalism. It presents criminals as 'Robin Hoods' – stealing from the rich and redistributing to the poor. Some sociologists, most notably Paul Gilroy, have suggested that young black criminals are politically motivated to commit crime by their discovery of the history of slavery and colonialism as well as by their experience of racism and police harassment.

Evaluation of the 'New Criminology'

- Left Realists (see pp 26–27) have criticized the New Criminology for over-romanticizing working-class criminals as 'Robin Hoods' who are fighting capitalism by stealing from the rich and giving to the poor.
- The reality of crime is that most victims of working-class and black crime are themselves working class and black. It is suggested that Taylor *et al.* do not take the effects of this type of crime on working-class victims seriously.
- It is difficult to imagine a political motive underpinning crimes such as domestic violence, rape and child abuse.
- Roger Hopkins Burke (2005) concludes that Marxism and the 'New Criminology' are too general to explain crime and too idealistic to tackle crime practically.

Marxist subcultural theory

Some Marxists have focused on working-class deviant or 'spectacular' youth subcultures such as 'teddy boys' (1950s), 'mods' and 'rockers' (1960s), 'skinheads' (1970s), 'punks' (late 1970s) and 'ravers' (1980s/1990s). They suggest that these can be seen as a form of ideological resistance to the dominant adult value system shaped by middle-class and capitalist values.

Key study

The Birmingham Centre for Contemporary Cultural Studies (CCCS) argued that youth subcultural styles should be read as a challenge to the class inequality that characterizes capitalist society.

For example, Phil Cohen (1972) studied 1970s skinheads and proposed that the skinhead style was a symbolic reaction to the decline of working-class communities, whose dress exaggerated working-class masculinity and aggression, while their anti-immigrant stance was a reaction to the decline of their white working-class neighbourhoods.

Dick Hebdige (1979) looked for the meanings behind the style of punk rockers in the late 1970s. He argues that punks set out to deliberately shock the establishment and society by adopting a style that reused ordinary objects such as bin-liners and safety pins, as well as deviant symbols such as the swastika and sexual bondage gear, to symbolically resist the dominant cultural values of the UK society of the time.

However, Hebdige notes that capitalist society quickly adapts to such challenges to its cultural dominance. He notes that punks and other youth subcultures are fairly short-lived because of **incorporation** – capitalism quickly commercializes aspects of youth cultural style, that is, puts them on sale, and strips them of their ideological significance so that they become just another consumer item.

Evaluation of Marxist subcultural theory

- Marxists neglect gender and ethnicity as influences on youth subculture.
- They underestimate the extent to which changes in youth culture are created by capitalism and shaped by consumerism.
- **Globalization**, particularly in the form of American cultural influences, is neglected.

Examiners' notes

The CCCS and Hebdige used mainly semiotic analysis to come to these conclusions. You need to be able to identify the strengths and weaknesses of this method.

Essential notes

'Skinheads' and 'punks' are not the only subcultures examined by the CCCS. They also looked at 'teddy boys' and 'mods' and came to similar conclusions. However, their ideas are supported by little **empirical** evidence.

Examiners' notes

Be aware of how the three types of Marxism – traditional, the New Criminology and Marxist subcultural theory – are related (e.g. all three accept that capitalism is a deeply unequal and exploitative system for the working class). Make sure you gain marks for evaluation by clearly identifying the differences.

Interactionist explanations of crime and deviance

Interactionist approaches to crime and deviance belong to the interpretivist tradition, which is interested in how people interpret and therefore socially construct the world around them. They are also interested in looking at how criminality develops in the **social interactions** between a potential deviant and **agents of social control**.

The relativity of deviance

Interactionists believe that 'normality' and 'deviance' are relative concepts because there is no universal or fixed agreement on how to define them. They point out that definitions of 'right' or 'wrong' behaviour differ according to social context. For example, nudity is fine in the privacy of the bathroom or bedroom but may be interpreted as a symptom of mental illness or criminality if persistently carried out in public.

Definitions of deviance change according to historical period; for example, homosexuality and suicide were defined as illegal activities until the 1960s. The definitions also change according to the cultural or subcultural context; for example, drinking alcohol is illegal in Saudi Arabia and disapproved of by some Muslims in the UK.

The interpretation of deviance

Interactionists believe that deviance is therefore a matter of interpretation. For example, society generally disapproves of killing people, although killing in self-defence and in battle are interpreted as necessary actions by society.

The social construction of deviance

Howard Becker argues that there is no such thing as a deviant act because no act is inherently criminal or deviant in itself, in all situations and at all times. Instead, it becomes criminal or deviant only when others label it as such.

Becker therefore argues that the social construction of deviance requires two activities. One group, which normally lacks power, acts in a particular way. Another group, with more power, responds negatively to it and defines and labels it as criminal. Therefore, for Becker, a deviant is simply someone to whom a label has been successfully applied; deviant behaviour is simply behaviour that people have labelled as such.

Becker notes that powerful groups create rules or laws in order to define what counts as crime and deviance, and labels those who fail to conform to these social controls as criminals or outlaws (outsiders).

The agents of social control

Becker notes that the agents of social control are made up of groups such as the police, the judiciary, social workers and probation workers. They work on behalf of politically powerful groups to label, and thus define, the behaviour of less powerful groups as being a problem. Consequently, the behaviour of the less powerful is subjected to greater surveillance and control by these social agencies.

Primary and secondary deviance

Edwin Lemert distinguishes between **primary deviance** and **secondary deviance**. Primary deviance refers to insignificant deviant acts that have not been publicly labelled. Such acts have little significance for a person's status or identity. As a result, primary deviants do not see themselves as deviant.

Secondary deviance is the result of societal reaction – of labelling. Being caught and publicly labelled as a criminal can involve being **stigmatized**, shunned and excluded from normal society. The criminal label can become a **master status**, which means that society interprets all actions and motives in the context of the label. For example, if a person is labelled a 'sex offender', the label shapes people's reactions to any other status the person has.

Secondary deviance is likely to provoke further hostile reactions from society such as prejudice and discrimination. For example, ex-cons may find it difficult to find legitimate employment. This may lead to a **deviant career** – the practical consequences of treating a person as a deviant may produce a **self-fulfilling prophecy** in that the labelled person may see him- or herself as deviant and act accordingly.

The person labelled a deviant may consequently seek comfort, sympathy, normality and status in a subculture of other people who have been branded with a similar label. This in turn may create further deviance.

Evaluation of labelling theory

- Labelling theory has shown that defining deviance is a complex process.
- It has shown that definitions of deviance are relative rather than fixed, universal or unchangeable.
- It was the first theory to draw sociological attention to the consequences of being labelled a deviant.

However:

- Peter Ackers argues that the deviant act is always more important than society's reaction. Deviants do not need to wait until a label is attached to know that what they are doing or have done is or was wrong.

- Labelling theory fails to explain the origin of deviance – it does not explain why people commit deviance in the first place, before they are labelled.

- Labelling theory implies that once someone is labelled, a deviant career is inevitable.

- Left Realists argue that it is guilty of over-romanticizing deviance and blaming the agencies of social control for causing crime. This ignores the real victims of crime.

Essential notes

Interactionist studies of crime have focused on how certain groups have come to be labelled as deviant by agents of social control such as the police and the mass media, and how such groups have reacted to the negative labels that have been applied to them. For example, Simon Holdaway's covert **participant observation** (conducted when he was a serving police officer) clearly shows that police officers negatively label and treat particular groups, notably ethnic minorities, and that this stereotyping may be responsible for their disproportionate appearance in the OCS.

Essential notes

The concept of power is central to the interactionist analysis. However, Marxists are critical of this theory, because interactionists are vague about the source of this power. Marxists argue that the power to label groups as criminal or deviant arises from the organization of capitalist society.

Essential notes

The concept of relative deprivation is important because it explains crime committed by a range of social groups. For example, even white-collar crime can be explained using this concept. However, this concept is clearly related to Merton's ideas – note that both individualism and relative deprivation are linked to the functionalist idea that people's main cultural goal should be material success. The notion that individualism undermines community comes straight from Durkheim.

Essential notes

These ideas are not new – note how similar they are to Cohen's ideas about status frustration.

Left Realist explanations of crime and deviance

The Left Realists John Lea and Jock Young aim to explain street crime committed by young people in urban areas. Their victim (or victimization) survey of inner-city London (the Islington Crime Survey (ICS)) suggested that working-class and black people, especially elderly women, have a realistic fear of street crime, because they reported that they are often the victims of such crime.

Lea and Young's explanation of why working-class and African-Caribbean young people commit crime revolves around three key concepts:

1. Relative deprivation

This refers to how deprived someone feels in relation to others, or compared with their own expectations. **Relative deprivation** can lead to crime when people feel resentment that, unfairly, others are better off than them. Lea and Young note that although people today are more prosperous compared with the past, they are more aware of their relative deprivation because of media and advertising, which raise everyone's expectations about standards of living.

Left Realism argues that working-class youth feel relatively deprived compared to middle-class youth while African-Caribbean youth compare themselves to white Britons with regard to life chances and opportunities such as living standards, access to consumer goods and income. These groups feel that they are relatively worse-off through no fault of their own. For example, young black Britons may feel that racism is holding them back.

Feelings of relative deprivation are heightened when combined with **individualism** – the pursuit of self-interest – and are likely to lead to criminal responses because individualism undermines the family and community values of mutual support, cooperation and selflessness. The informal social controls usually exercised by the family and community are weakened. As a result, anti-social behaviour, violence and crime increase.

2. Marginalization

Left Realists argue that young people often feel **marginalized** (they feel they have little or no power to change their situation) and frustrated – negative treatment by the police and the authorities may result in further feelings of hostility and resentment towards mainstream society, which may spill over into confrontation with authority.

3. Subculture

Some young working-class and black people who experience the feelings of relative deprivation and marginalization may form deviant subcultures. These subcultures react to the perception that society does not value them, by becoming involved in street crimes such as drug pushing, territorial gang violence, anti-social behaviour, joy-riding and mugging.

Left Realist solutions to crime

Left Realists argue that the only ways to cut crime are to:

1. Improve policing and control

Lea and Young argue that crime can only be reduced with the assistance of local communities. However, the military-style policing of inner-city communities, particularly black communities, has alienated local populations. For example, stop and search statistics in urban areas suggest that the police use racial profiling in their attempt to identify criminality; this has led to accusations of institutional racism. Lea and Young argue that the police need to regain the confidence of local communities so that people feel comfortable providing them with information about crime.

2. Deal with the deeper structural causes of crime

The main cause of crime is the deeply unequal nature of capitalist society and its inequalities in income, wealth and opportunity, which have undermined social cohesion and produced a culture of envy, frustration and hostility. Lea and Young argue that crime can only be reduced or eliminated by improving people's opportunities to achieve a decent standard of living. This can only be done by reducing income and wealth inequalities, by creating jobs for all and by improving housing and the environment of the inner cities and council estates.

However, Young has criticized governments of all political viewpoints for failing to tackle the basic inequalities which cause the insecurity, relative deprivation, marginalization and exclusion that probably fuel most crime.

Evaluation of Left Realism

- Gordon Hughes argues that Left Realists have drawn our attention to the brutalizing and unromantic reality of inner-city street crimes.
- They have also highlighted the effect of crime on victims.
- Left Realists have also shown clearly that most victims of crime are members of deprived groups – which most theories of crime have neglected.

However:

- There is little empirical evidence to support the view that young working-class or black criminals interpret their realities in the way described by Lea and Young.
- Lea and Young do not explain why the majority of working-class and African-Caribbean youth do not turn to crime.
- The theory only focuses on subcultural criminal responses and does not explain crimes such as burglary, which is committed by individuals rather than gangs.
- It also focuses exclusively on street crime and largely ignores white-collar and corporate crime.
- It fails to account for opportunist crime committed by adults.

Essential notes

It is important to understand that subcultures do not have to be deviant. Some subcultures may be based around sport or religion, and channel feelings of frustration into positive areas.

Right Realist explanations of crime and deviance

Right Realists see crime, especially street crime, as a real and growing problem that undermines social cohesion and can destroy social communities. Right Realists believe that people are selfish, individualistic and greedy. So, they assume that people are 'naturally' inclined towards criminal behaviour if it can further their interests and/or if there is little chance of being caught.

Types of Right Realism

There are three main aspects to Right Realist theories of crime.

1. 'Underclass' theory

Charles Murray suggests that in the USA and the UK, a distinct lower-class subculture exists, below the working class – an '**underclass**' – which subscribes to deviant and criminal values rather than mainstream values and transmits this deficient culture to their children via socialization.

David Marsland argues that the welfare state is responsible for the emergence of this 'underclass' because **welfare dependency** has undermined people's sense of commitment and obligation to support one another. People belonging to the 'underclass' are allegedly work-shy, preferring to live off state benefits rather than work.

Murray sees the 'underclass' as generally lacking in moral values, especially commitment to marriage and family life. A large percentage of 'underclass' children are brought up by single mothers who are allegedly often inadequate and irresponsible parents. Absent fathers mean that boys lack paternal discipline and male role models, so young males may turn to other, often delinquent, role models on the street and gain status through crime rather than supporting their families by doing a steady job. These young males are also generally hostile towards the police and authority.

As a result, Right Realists see this alleged 'underclass' as the main cause of crime in recent years in inner-city areas and on council estates.

Examiners' notes

'Underclass' is a loaded term and is therefore difficult to research. Questionnaire surveys aimed at the poor suggest that, with regard to jobs, they subscribe to the same types of beliefs as do most other people, and that unemployment, poverty and debt have a negative effect on self-esteem and health.

Key study

Simon Charlesworth used **ethnographic research** to investigate the effects of poverty and unemployment on people living on a council estate in Rotherham, South Yorkshire.

He took a flat on the estate and used both participant observation and conversational interviews to document the daily lives of the poor. He found that:

- Miserable economic conditions had a profound negative effect on physical and mental health.
- Many unemployed people suffered from depression.
- Many people felt robbed of identity and value because they did not have a job.
- Although some people were motivated by their conditions to commit crime, most did not.
- There were few signs of the anti-social 'underclass' identified by Murray.

2. Rational choice theory

Clarke (1980) argues that the decision to commit crime is a choice based on a rational calculation of the likely consequences. If the rewards of crime outweigh its costs or if the rewards of crime appear to be greater than those of non-criminal behaviour, then people will be more likely to offend.

Right Realists argue that currently, the perceived costs of crime are low, so the crime rate has increased. Criminals foresee little risk of being caught.

3. Control theories

Travis Hirschi argues that people are generally rational in terms of their actions and choices – they weigh up the 'costs' and 'benefits' of their behaviour, and on this basis, they make choices about their actions.

Hirschi also argues that most people do not commit crimes, as they have four controls in their lives. The cost of crime (being caught and punished) outweighs the economic and personal benefits. The four controls are:

1. Attachment – being committed to family relationships, which may be threatened by involvement in criminality
2. Commitment – people may have invested years in education or in building up a career, business or home, all of which may be lost and wasted if a person is involved in crime
3. Involvement – people may be actively involved in community life; for example, as volunteers, magistrates, parent governors at local schools; respect and reputation would be lost if they engaged in crime
4. Belief – people may have been brought up to be strongly committed to beliefs in rules, discipline and respect for others and the law.

Hirschi suggests that these controls prevent many people from turning to crime. As people get older, they begin to acquire these controls. Younger people usually have less to lose in terms of things like attachment. For them, respect and reputation might even be enhanced by criminality.

Evaluation of Right Realism

- John Rex and Sally Tomlinson reject the idea of the 'underclass' as a deviant subculture that is voluntarily unemployed and devoted to criminal behaviour. They point out that poverty is often caused by factors beyond the control of the poor, for example, global recession and government policies.
- There is no convincing empirical evidence that the 'underclass' as a distinct subculture with distinctive values and behaviour exists.
- Stan Cohen argues that **New Right** thinking leads to class inequalities in victimization – the rich live in 'paranoid fortresses' or 'gated communities' guarded by technology and private security forces, thus displacing crime to poorer, less protected areas.
- Right Realism overstates the rationality of criminals. For example, it is doubtful whether violent crime is underpinned by rationality.

Essential notes

Like Durkheim, Hirschi is more interested in why most people conform, rather than why they commit crimes. Consequently, his theory is more about social control than about criminality. However, his theory implies that young people, ethnic minorities and members of the 'underclass' are more likely to commit crime, as they are more likely to lack the controls of attachment, commitment, involvement and belief.

Examiners' notes

Hirschi's ideas lack empirical evidence to support them. Think about how questionnaires or interviews might be designed and used to investigate the validity of these ideas.

Examiners' notes

Think about a comparative approach – what two groups might be selected to take part in this research? How might we **operationalize** Hirschi's concepts of attachment, commitment, involvement and belief?

Feminism, crime and deviance

Some feminist criminologists accept that women commit less crime than men. Diana Leonard believes that the major explanation for this fact is that women are more likely to conform to rules and social controls than men. However, there are signs that this commitment to the rules may be undermined by social class and age. There are six feminist explanations as to why females commit less crime than males.

1. Differential socialization

Early feminist explanations focused on differences in the socialization of males and females. Both Carol Smart and Ann Oakley suggested that males are socialized into aggressive, self-seeking and individualistic behaviour that may make them more disposed to taking risks and committing criminal acts. On the other hand, females are socialized into a potentially less criminal set of values and norms that stress cooperation, tenderness and caring for others.

2. Differential controls

Frances Heidensohn argues that females are generally more conformist because patriarchal society imposes greater control over their behaviour. This can be illustrated in various ways:

- Smart notes that girls are more strictly supervised by their parents, especially outside the home. Angela McRobbie and Jenny Garber concluded that teenage girls' lives revolve around a **bedroom culture**, so they are more likely than boys to socialize with friends in the home rather than on the streets or other public places.
- Sue Lees notes that girls are more likely to be controlled, in that they may fear acquiring a 'bad' reputation. She notes that boys in schools often use verbalized sexual labels such as 'slag' to control girls. Girls may therefore steer clear of deviant behaviour to avoid these labels.
- Heidensohn notes that women are more likely to be controlled by their family roles as wives and mothers – they consequently have little time or opportunity for illegal activity.
- Women are less likely to be in public places in which crime and deviance normally occur especially at night, because of the threat or fear of male violence or the fear of acquiring a bad reputation.

3. Rational choices

Pat Carlen notes that working-class females may commit crimes because they lack the four controls that prevent most people from committing crimes (see p 29).

Carlen argues that criminal women are often women who have failed to gain qualifications and find legitimate work. They often live in poverty and are dependent on benefits. Their attachment to family life may be weak because they have been abused by family members, run away from home and/or spent time in care. Many have run away from home and lived rough on the streets. Carlen argues that many of these criminal women come to the rational conclusion that crime is the only route to a decent standard of living. Getting a criminal record reinforces future criminal behaviour because it makes commitment to a conventional job and family life even

Examiners' notes

Carlen conducted unstructured tape-recorded interviews with 39 working women, aged 15 to 46, who had been convicted of a range of crimes. At the times of the interviews, 20 were in custody. What problems of **reliability** might have occurred because of the method used? Why might the research design have produced high levels of validity in terms of the data generated by the interviews?

less likely. However, critics of this theory suggest that Carlen fails to explain why many women in poverty choose *not* to commit crime.

4. Feminization of poverty

Some feminist sociologists suggest that poverty has become feminized in the last 20 years, as women have become increasingly more likely than men to experience low pay and benefits. Consequently, some types of crime dominated by females, notably shoplifting and social security fraud, may be a reaction to poverty. Sandra Walklate notes that shoplifting and prostitution are often motivated by economic necessity, for example, to provide children with food, toys and clothes.

5. Liberation theory

Freda Adler argues that as society becomes less patriarchal, so women's crime rates will rise. In other words, women's liberation from patriarchy will lead to a new type of female criminal because they will have greater opportunity and confidence to commit crime.

- Between 1981 and 1997 the number of under-18 girls convicted of violent offences in England and Wales doubled – from 65 per 100 000 to 135 per 100 000.
- A Demos survey of 2000 UK women aged 18 to 24 found that one in eight respondents believed it was acceptable to use physical violence to get something they really wanted.

Key study

A questionnaire survey of teenage girls in Glasgow carried out by Michele Burman *et al.* found that 98.5% of girls had witnessed, first-hand, some form of interpersonal physical violence; 70% had witnessed, first-hand, five or more such incidents. Nearly two-thirds knew someone who had been physically hurt or injured by violence; 41% had experienced someone deliberately hitting, punching, or kicking them. Ten per cent of the girls described themselves as 'violent' and 10% reported having committed seven or more types of physically violent acts such as punching, kicking and hitting with an object.

Other critics point out that economic changes have benefitted mainly middle-class women. There are few signs of these women being involved in white-collar or corporate crime. Most female offenders are working class and are probably motivated by many of the same factors that motivate working-class men, for example, poverty and the feelings of humiliation, powerlessness, envy and hostility that accompany a marginalized position in society.

6. Postmodern perspectives

Hazel Croall looks at female crime from a **postmodern** perspective and suggests that teenage girls are usually motivated to commit crime by three inter-related factors:

- A drug habit (which often leads to prostitution and shoplifting).
- The excitement that often accompanies the act of committing crime.
- The **conspicuous consumption** of goods such as designer label clothing, which are often the target of shoplifting.

Examiners' notes

Self-report studies are a type of questionnaire used to investigate gender differences in committed crime. Campbell's self-report study found that the ratio of male crime to female crime is 1.5 to 1 rather than 7 to 1. However, the findings of such surveys are often undermined by over-reporting, under-reporting, ethical problems and the difficulty of finding a **representative** sample.

Essential notes

The empirical studies of territorial street gangs operating in UK cities in the 21st century by John Pitts and Keith Kintrea, highlight the **hyper-masculine** aspect of gang culture focused on the search for respect and status, which they claim is responsible for much gun and knife crime in urban areas.

Explanations of gender differences in crime rates – masculinity

Until fairly recently, the idea that masculinity exerted a major influence on crime was generally neglected. Feminism was the first theory to draw criminological attention to the role of **gender-role socialization** in the social construction of crime. Oakley, for example, suggested that gender-role socialization in the UK, especially in working-class families, might result in boys and men subscribing to values that potentially overlap with criminality.

Oakley's ideas were developed by James Messerschmidt, who argued that boys in the UK are socialized into a **hegemonic** masculine value system that stresses differences from women, and particular masculine goals that need to be achieved in order to become a 'real man'. These goals include:

- The need to acquire respect from other men in order to maintain reputation.
- Having power, authority and control over others.
- The **objectification of women** and the celebration of masculine virility through promiscuity.
- Toughness expressed through aggression, confrontation and force.
- Territorial loyalty and honour expressed through being part of a larger group.
- Being emotionally hard and not expressing weakness by showing feelings.
- Being anti-authority, by claiming individuality and self-reliance.
- Taking risks and living life on the edge.
- Seeking pleasure, thrills and excitement to compensate for the boredom of work or unemployment.

Messerschmidt argues that working-class youth's experience of education is often one of under-achievement. Anti-social subcultures are constructed and organized around the achievement of hegemonic masculine values to compensate for the negative experience of school. These gangs operate both inside and outside of school. However, Messerschmidt notes that this need to live out masculine values is not confined to working-class youth and men. He notes that middle-class men may be motivated by this masculine value system to commit white-collar and corporate crime.

Examiners' notes

Student responses to essay questions on gender and crime tend to over-focus on the reasons why women do or do not commit crime. To maximize your marks, make sure you make reference to how male crime might be shaped by masculinity.

However Messerschmidt's analysis has been criticized because he fails to explain why not all men use crime to accomplish hegemonic masculine goals. The majority are law-abiding citizens. Furthermore, there is debate as to whether masculinity is a major cause of crime or whether it is merely one way in which crime is expressed. For example, is it just an expression of toughness rather than being a cause of crime?

Key study

Simon Winlow's study: The changing nature of masculinity

Winlow's study of masculinity in Sunderland suggests that most working-class men traditionally expressed their masculine values through the work they did through their domestic roles as breadwinner and head of household and through their leisure time, which focused mainly on drinking in pubs. Opportunities to get involved in crime were fairly low and violence, when it occurred, which was fairly rare, was shaped by masculine competition for respect and status or for the attention of women.

However, the mass unemployment of the 1980s experienced in industrial communities such as Sunderland meant that men could no longer express their masculinity through their work or by being the breadwinner. Economic change often meant that women became the breadwinners. Winlow notes that young men, in particular, experienced long-term unemployment after leaving school and became dependent on benefits. Winlow argues that these young men increasingly value violence, as it offers a release from boredom and access to status. In this world, the gang becomes all-important because it provides thrills, protection, mutual support, friendship, prestige, and income to buy fashionable clothes, alcohol and drugs.

Winlow suggests that the nature of criminal opportunity has also changed because of these economic changes. Criminality is now an **entrepreneurial concern** – a means of making money. Crime and violence have become careers in themselves. For example, money can now be made:

- illegitimately, through protection rackets, dealing in drugs and/or stolen cars and loan sharking
- legitimately, by being a bouncer or a security consultant.

Postmodern studies of masculinity and crime

Jackson Katz argues that young males commit crime for the pleasure or thrill that is derived from the risk of being caught or having power over others. Katz refers to these thrills as transgressions.

Stephen Lyng suggests that much of crime is **edgework**, as it is located on the edge between the thrill of getting away with it and the potential danger and uncertainty of being captured and punished.

In this sense, crime is a form of gambling, providing pleasure and thrills. It allows young men who have little economic security to exercise a form of control over their lives.

Katz also notes that violence, in terms of thrill and power exercised over others, is rational in the context of achieving the goals of hegemonic masculinity.

Essential notes

It is not just young males who are motivated by the excitement and danger associated with crime. Some criminologists, notably Croall, suggest female teenage crime might also be the product of this need for thrills.

Ethnicity and crime

African-Caribbean people and to a lesser extent, Asian people, are over-represented in the official crime statistics (OCS) and in the prison population (see pp 14–15).

The ethnic minority prison population has doubled in a decade – from 11 332 in 1998 to 22 421 in 2008. Over a similar period, the overall number of prisoners rose by less than two-thirds.

Most of these prisoners are male. For example, in 2007, there were 19 658 male ethnic minority prisoners constituting 26% of the total prison population. Thirty-six per cent of 15- to 18-year-old men held in youth custody in England and Wales are from black or other ethnic minority groups. Ethnic minority women are also over-represented in the criminal justice system. In 2009, 29% of the female prison population was made up of ethnic minority women.

In 2008–09, black and mixed-race people made up 17.8% of the prison population, while Asians and Chinese people constituted 8.9%. Muslims made up 12% of the prison population.

Sociological explanations of ethnic minority crime
Demographic explanations

Morris argues that according to the OCS most crime is committed by young people and that ethnic minority groups include a higher proportion of young people who have committed crimes than the white population. However, if this was the case, young Asians would also be over-represented, as the majority of Asians in the UK are under 30 years old. However, this group does not feature as heavily as young black Britons.

Interpretivist critiques of the criminal justice system

Interpretivist sociologists argue that crime statistics do not tell us much about black or Asian criminality. They simply tell us about their involvement with the criminal justice system. The evidence suggests that the OCS may not be a true record of ethnic minority crime; rather that the OCS may simply reflect levels of discrimination towards ethnic minorities.

Coretta Phillips and Ben Bowling (2007) argue that since the 1970s the black community has been subjected to oppressive military-style policing, which has resulted in the over-policing of these communities, reflected in the excessive police use of stop and search. Statistics on police stop and search, released in March 2010, reveal that the police stop and search black Britons six times more than white Britons and Asians twice as often as white Britons.

Various observational studies of police-suspect interaction suggest that the decisions of police officers to stop, search and arrest young African-Caribbean males are based on negative racial profiling or stereotyping. Simon Holdaway argues that police canteen culture is still characterized by racist language, jokes and banter and this racist culture often underpins the decision to stop black Britons. The MacPherson Report into the death of black teenager Stephen Lawrence found that the London Metropolitan Police was guilty of 'institutional racism' in its failure to tackle such discrimination. In 2008, the Metropolitan Black Police Association warned people from ethnic minorities not to join the police force because of the hostile and racist atmosphere at many London police stations.

Key study

P. A. J. Waddington *et al.* watched CCTV footage of police officers and interviewed officers about their stop and search activities.

They found that although a disproportionate number of ethnic minority youth were stopped, this was a realistic reflection of the type of people who were on the streets at night in high crime areas.

In other words, police stop and search policies are not shaped by racial prejudice and discrimination, but by the composition of the local population.

Research indicates the possibility of some bias in the judicial process. C. Sharp and T. Budd observed in 2005 that black youth have lower offence levels compared to white youth, but are more likely to be arrested, and convicted. Moreover, compared to white youth, black and Asian offenders are more likely to be charged rather than cautioned and remanded in custody rather than bailed. Roger Hood's study of criminal courts in the West Midlands concluded that young African-Caribbean males were more likely than white youth to receive custodial sentences for similar offences.

Self-report studies such as the 'Offending, Crime and Justice Survey' carried out in 2003 seem to support the view that the criminal justice system may be institutionally racist because they consistently show that white Britons have a higher rate of offending than black Britons. Moreover, those offences such as violence and drug-selling, which are stereotypically associated with black youth, are more likely to be committed by white youth.

Phillips and Bowling suggest that this negative treatment by the criminal justice system may lead some members of black communities to feel hostile towards the police. They note that young black Britons commit more street robbery than other ethnic groups and suggest that this is a product of the negative labelling that stems from constantly being stopped and searched by the police. Crime is an expression of the hostility they feel towards the police. In other words, police labelling produces a self-fulfilling prophecy, as young black Britons live up to the stereotype of potential criminals.

Examiners' notes

If you are required to write a general essay on the merits of interactionism or labelling theory, you can use Phillips and Bowling's findings on the policing of ethnic minorities to illustrate the labelling process.

Key study

Ernest Cashmore, using the ideas of Merton, argues that young African-Caribbeans in Britain are culturally encouraged like everybody else to pursue material success, but their structural opportunities are blocked by factors such as failing inner-city schools, unemployment and racism. Young black Britons experience anomie – they are aware that their situation arises from being black in a predominantly white society.

They turn to street crime, which Merton described as 'innovation' (see p 17) – and justify their criminal activities on the grounds that they are rejecting white society because it has failed them.

Examiners' notes

Use Cashmore's ideas to illustrate the functionalist theory of crime and deviance.

☞ **This topic continues on the next two pages**

However, Left Realists note that these blocked opportunities are experienced by the majority of African-Caribbeans, but Cashmore fails to explain why only a small proportion of young black Britons actually turn to crime.

Neo-Marxist theory

Neo-Marxist Stuart Hall claims that the criminalization of black people began in the 1970s when the police selectively released statistics suggesting that young black Britons were more likely than other groups to be responsible for street robbery or mugging, and that white Britons were most likely to be their victims. This initiated a moral panic, which effectively labelled the young African-Caribbean population as a folk devil, or criminal threat.

According to Hall, Britain in the early 1970s was undergoing a crisis of capitalism because unemployment was fairly high, industrial disputes were common and riots, street protests and violent demonstrations were threatening the **hegemony**, or cultural dominance, of the ruling capitalist class or **bourgeoisie**.

However, the moral panic focused on mugging came to play a crucial ideological function for the capitalist ruling class in two ways:

1. It divided the working class by encouraging racist attitudes – white working-class people were encouraged by the media, the police and politicians to view the black working class as a problem. This distracted members of the working class from the real cause of their problems – the mismanagement of capitalism by the ruling class.
2. It justified the introduction of more aggressive policing, particularly stop and search, and riot squads that could be used against other 'problem' groups such as strikers, protesters and demonstrators.

In Hall's view, the OCS, which show high levels of black criminality, are socially manufactured by a repressive racist state for ideological reasons.

Key study

Paul Gilroy on crime committed by young African-Caribbeans

Paul Gilroy argues that crime committed by young African-Caribbeans is political, because it is frequently motivated by their interpretation of their position in UK society.

He argues that much black street crime is a conscious and deliberate reaction and resistance to the anger of young black Britons at the way white society has historically treated black people via slavery and colonialism, and the institutional racism of everyday life represented by police harassment and employer discrimination.

Examiners' notes

You can use the work of Hall and Gilroy to illustrate an essay question on Marxist explanations of crime and deviance.

However, the fact that most young and adult African-Caribbeans are law-abiding citizens, challenges the view that crime is part of an anti-colonial or anti-racist struggle. There is also no empirical evidence that black youth have the political motives that Gilroy identifies. Left Realists note that most black crime is committed against other black Britons, rather than white Britons.

Left Realism

Lea and Young attempted to explain street crime committed by both working-class white and black youth. They suggest four concepts are central to understanding why some members of ethnic minorities commit crime:

	Concept	Description
1.	Relative deprivation	The poor, whose lives are undermined by social and economic factors beyond their control such as racism, feel deprived of material possessions, especially compared with what they see (e.g. in the media or advertising)
2.	Individualism	People are encouraged, especially by the mass media and celebrity culture, to pursue self-interest at the expense of the community
3.	Marginalization	Ethnic minorities may feel frustrated and hostile because they have very little power to change the situation
4.	Subculture	People are more likely to commit crime if they find other like-minded individuals who want to aspire to material success and/or who share their anger and hostility towards society. As Pitts notes, this may mean subcultural responses such as territorial street gangs involved in violence or drug-pushing

Table 10
Lea and Young's four concepts, central to understanding why some members of ethnic minorities commit crime

Tony Sewell – triple quandary theory

In Sewell's triple **quandary** theory, he identifies three risk factors that are responsible for the relatively high levels of crime among African-Caribbean boys.

1. They feel that they cannot relate to mainstream culture because they believe, for example, that teachers, police officers and employers are racist and therefore working against their interests.
2. They are very influenced by the media's emphasis on conspicuous consumption – the idea that identity and status are dependent on material things such as designer labels and jewellery.
3. Many African-Caribbean boys are brought up in single-parent families. The absence of a father means that they lack the positive male role models that could encourage a more positive view of society.

Sewell argues that these three quandaries create anxiety for black boys, which is resolved by constructing subcultures or gangs. These gangs become the arena in which young black males gain respect and status from their peers by engaging in hyper-masculine activity such as violence, as well as conspicuous consumption from the proceeds of crime.

Essential notes

Sewell takes a multi-dimensional approach to black street crime. He argues that society needs to take some responsibility for racism and for exaggerating material needs through the media. However, he is also regarded as controversial because he believes that black people need to take more responsibility for their actions.

Social class and crime

The official crime statistics (OCS) indicate that people from working-class backgrounds are more likely to commit crimes than those from middle-class backgrounds (see p 15). An examination of the employment status of convicted offenders suggests that over 80% are from the manual labour or working-class sectors.

The functionalist, Robert Merton (see pp 16–17) suggests that the working classes are more likely to commit crime because of the organization of capitalism, which places huge emphasis on the goal of material success and wealth. Those at the bottom of society – the working class and the poor – experience a gap between this goal and the institutional means available. Educationally, they tend to underachieve and so are unable to access the jobs that would lead them to achieve material success. The lack of education blocks opportunities, which may lead to anomie or frustration. Although most members of working-class society conform and aspire to achieve goals by conventional means, some may turn to deviant or criminal means such as 'innovation' (for example, street crimes such as robbery, burglary or dealing in drugs) to achieve material success. Some working-class people may not be able to cope with failure, and may turn to deviance such as 'retreatism', in the form of alcoholism, drug addiction or suicide.

However, despite the usefulness of Merton's analysis, it has some problems:

- Surveys suggest that the working class may not share the meritocratic ideal that one day they will be well-off materially – they may be realistic about their limits of achievement.
- Marxist Laurie Taylor dismisses Merton's theory because Merton fails to acknowledge that laws are actually made by the capitalist class in order to protect their economic interests rather than the interests of all people.
- Merton's theory does not adequately explain domestic forms of violence.

Despite these criticisms, sociologists such as William Sumner, Robert Reiner and Jock Young suggest that in the UK today, money and celebrity status have become the main sources of status. However, there is also a 'chaos of reward' in that extravagant and often unmerited rewards are paid to those at the top of society, while those at the bottom of society get poorer. Reiner suggests that Merton's concepts of blocked opportunities and anomie may explain the frustration of these poorer sections of society who may be turning to violent crimes such as street robbery to express their resentment at their lack of opportunity.

Albert Cohen (see p 18) attempted to explain working-class juvenile gang crimes such as vandalism, hooliganism and territorial violence. He argued that the main cause of this type of deviance was 'status frustration', which was caused by schools denying working-class boys status by placing them in bottom groups. Supposedly, the boys react to their frustration by forming anti-school (counter) cultures, which allocate status to one another on the basis of anti-school delinquency. This is carried over into leisure time. However, Paul Willis notes that Cohen does not explain why most working-class youths actually conform at school; and feminists complain that he ignores female delinquency.

There is some evidence from modern studies of territorial gang violence conducted by John Pitts and Keith Kintrea, that the acquisition of a hyper-masculine status through the use of violence may be a major motivation for the behaviour of gang members. Boys who live in inner-city areas that are characterized by failing schools, high unemployment and poverty may interpret education and society as denying them status and so seek to attain it through membership of street gangs.

Miller (see p 19) claims that working-class delinquency is simply the result of young people exaggerating already deviant working-class values (focal concerns) such as masculinity, toughness, drinking and risk-taking, especially at the weekend, to compensate for the boredom of school, jobs and unemployment. This exaggeration consequently brings them into contact with the police and other agents of social control. However, Matza notes that most youth drift in and out of delinquency but few are committed to it.

Labelling theorists (see pp 24–25) such as Howard Becker argue that the working class are no more deviant than the middle class but the powerful make rules to criminalize their activities. The police (acting on behalf of the powerful) label the young and black working class as potentially criminal, or suspicious, and therefore tend to stop and arrest them more often.

Marxists (see pp 20–21) such as David Gordon argue that working-class crime is a rational and realistic response to class inequality. Gordon argues that working-class people are alienated by the fact that in the modern UK the rich are getting richer and the poor are getting poorer. Moreover, they can see that the law and the police protect the interests of the powerful and that the law is selectively enforced. White-collar and corporate crimes are not pursued as vigorously as working-class crimes. For example, benefit fraud, which is committed mainly by the poor, is treated more harshly than tax fraud, which is committed mainly by the wealthy, despite the latter being more costly to the nation. See pp 20–21 for more detail on white-collar crime and corporate crime.

Left Realists, John Lea and Jock Young (see pp 26–27) argue that working-class juvenile delinquency is caused by a combination of relative deprivation (they feel economically and socially deprived compared to their middle-class peers) and marginalization (they feel powerless and picked on, especially by the police, and frustrated because they cannot change their situation). Some people compensate by turning to deviant subcultures.

Essential notes

There is a growing contemporary literature on British street gangs and territorial violence, which suggests that Cohen's emphasis on status is valid.

Examiners' notes

In terms of evaluation, labelling theory fails to explain why working-class people may be motivated to commit crime. Instead, it strongly implies that they are victims of agents of social control who label them as being suspicious or criminal for no good reason.

Essential notes

Gordon suggests that on the whole most poor people conform despite the fact that they struggle to survive on a daily basis. Other Marxists argue that this is because ideological apparatuses such as the mass media and education successfully socialize them into conformity.

Essential notes

Left Realism theory is essentially a hybrid of previous theories. The concept of relative deprivation is similar to Merton's concepts of blocked opportunities and anomie, whereas marginalization is essentially saying that they are experiencing Cohen's status frustration. There is also a focus on social class inequality and racism.

Essential notes

Ecological theory is closely related to both functionalism and subcultural theory, in that the residents of inner-city areas are more likely to experience blocked opportunities and subsequent strain and anomie. Furthermore, delinquent subcultures focused on territorial street gangs are more likely to emerge in inner cities in the search for status. Illegitimate opportunity structures are also more likely to be available in inner-city areas.

Geographical location and crime

The official crime statistics (OCS) show that recorded crime is not evenly distributed between geographical areas. It is higher in urban areas than in rural areas, and higher in inner cities and on council estates compared to suburban areas of cities and towns (see p 15). British Crime Survey (BCS) data suggests that people who live in rural areas worry less about crime than city residents. Urban dwellers are also more likely to perceive their areas as experiencing high levels of anti-social behaviour.

Some theories have therefore examined the environment or **ecology** of towns and cities in order to explain crime. During the 1920s, the Chicago School of sociologists looked at the relationship between criminality and the urban environment, and attempted to explain why crime rates were so high in cities.

Clifford Shaw and Henry McKay, who examined the organization of American cities such as Chicago, observed that most are arranged into distinct neighbourhoods or zones, each with its own distinctive subcultural values and lifestyles. Shaw and McKay paid particular attention to 'zone two', the inner city, naming it the **zone of transition**. It was characterized by cheap rented housing, poverty, high numbers of immigrants and high crime rates. They noted that 'relative' crime rates in the inner city were similar over a number of years, even though the immigrant groups dominating the zone had changed. This indicated that the high crime rates were not due to the specific cultural characteristics of specific immigrant groups.

Shaw and McKay concluded that the constant movement of people in and out of these areas prevented the formation of stable communities and a sense of social control. Instead, it produced a state of **social disorganization**, with little sense of community. As a result, people were unlikely to feel a sense of duty and obligation to one another, and so felt little guilt about committing crimes against their neighbours. This theory, which is influenced by Durkheim's theory of anomie, therefore links rising crime rates to the decline of community.

Shaw and McKay note that areas of social disorganization produce subcultures of delinquency, which culturally transmit criminal behaviour, skills and values from one generation to the next. This **cultural transmission** ensures that young criminals, whether male or female, learn criminal skills and traditions from the older generation, and that social disorganization is reproduced and maintained. Edwin Sutherland's idea of **differential association** is a very similar concept. He suggests that cultural behaviour is shaped by those around them. If people who live in a socially disorganized urban area frequently associate with people who make their living from crime, then the choice to pursue a criminal career may not be a difficult option.

Gordon Marshall *et al.* suggest that zones of transition made up of sink estates and deteriorating inner-city areas can be spotted in UK cities. They argue that these areas lack any sense of community spirit or social control. As a result, some people feel free to commit crime at will. Such disorganization is reinforced by the state's failure to address **social problems** such as unemployment, poverty, poor mental health, and drug and alcohol abuse.

Evaluation of ecological explanations

- Shaw and McKay's analysis of crime is tautological, meaning that it is unclear which comes first, the crime or the social disorganization. For example, social disorganization might be the effect of high crime rates rather than the cause of them.
- The majority of people living in areas with high crime rates choose not to commit crime despite being stereotyped by Shaw and McKay's theory. However, although children and teenagers may sometimes be involved in delinquency, the evidence suggests that there is very little adolescent commitment to the notion of gangs or subcultures in most urban areas and that involvement for most is either non-existent or fleeting, which means that they might drift in and out on the fringes of these subcultures. This challenges the concepts of cultural transmission and differential association.
- The ecological approach neglects the fact that evidence for inner-city crime tends to come from the OCS, which are socially constructed and may tell sociologists more about policing than about crime and criminals. For example, the disproportionate amount of urban crime found in the OCS may be due to the military-style over-policing of these areas and the excessive use of stop and search.
- John Baldwin and A. E. Bottoms blame **tipping** – the way local people interpret social changes in their area – for urban decline. If law-abiding people perceive their area to be changing for the worse because of anti-social behaviour, they may move out and be replaced by the friends and relatives of those responsible for the anti-social behaviour. If the anti-social families outweigh the respectable families, the area has tipped and will be viewed by the police, local council and community as a 'problem'.

Essential notes

This critique of the ecological approach comes from an interpretivist perspective and suggests that some groups appear more in the OCS because those with power are able to label them as criminals.

Key study

Dick Hobbs *et al.* identify what they call a **night-time economy**.

They found that since the 1990s the number of clubs and pubs in city centres has grown rapidly, catering primarily for the leisure needs of younger people. Vast numbers of young people come to city centres within a very narrow time frame to seek pleasure through drinking and socializing.

Later research by Hobbs *et al.* illustrates this point. In Manchester, around 75 000 people are out on Friday and Saturday nights and about 75% of all violent incidents in urban areas occur at the weekend between 9 pm and 3 am, often fuelled by drink and drugs. There are only about 30 police officers to control the 'night-time economy' in Manchester. The main responsibility for social control has passed to private security companies in the form of door staff or 'bouncers'.

Examiners' notes

Illustrate this fact with examples of juvenile delinquency *or* examples of the types of conventional crimes committed mainly by young people.

Essential notes

Cohen was very influenced by Robert Merton. His theory uses Mertonian ideas; for example, that working-class boys' desire for status is blocked by the school and society. In other words, they experience a strain between their goals and the means of achieving those goals.

Essential notes

Jonathan Smith conducted a study of personal robbery using police crime reports and witness statements and concluded that the main motives for robbery were financial advantage and to enhance personal reputation and status.

Examiners' notes

In terms of evaluation, labelling theory fails to explain why young people may be motivated to commit crime. Instead, it implies strongly that they are victims of agents of social control who label them as being suspicious or criminal for no good reason.

Age and crime

Crime committed by young people is known as juvenile delinquency. The official crime statistics (OCS) suggest that roughly half of all crime is committed by 14- to 18-year-olds (see p 14).

Albert Cohen (see p 18) was the first sociologist to attempt to explain juvenile delinquency. In the 1950s, he focused on collective gang crime such as vandalism, hooliganism and territorial violence in the USA. His analysis focused on why working-class males were attracted to collective and malicious forms of deviant behaviour. He argued that the main cause of this type of deviance was 'status frustration', caused by:

- working-class parents failing to adequately socialize their children into the values and skills required for success in education
- schools denying such boys status by putting them in bottom groups

He argued that the boys react to their frustration by forming anti-school (counter) cultures that allocate status to one another on the basis of anti-school delinquency, which is carried over into leisure time. Cohen is therefore blaming both working-class culture and society – the latter because schools fail to give these youngsters what they want, notably, status.

Some contemporary studies of territorial violence in the UK, which has resulted in dozens of deaths from gun and knife crime, support the view that gaining status or respect is central to gang identity today. Keith Kintrea's study of gang violence in six UK cities concluded that participation in territorial conflict, which often involved carrying weapons and frequent violent confrontation with rivals from other areas, produced a heightened sense of masculinity and 'respect' or status from other gang members.

However, labelling theorists such as Howard Becker (see p 24) argue that deviance is a relative concept. The activities of the young are no more deviant than the activities of older people. However, older people such as parents, teachers and politicians are more powerful than younger people, and so make the rules. These rules tend to label the activities of younger people as deviant. Labelling theory argues that the police, who act on behalf of the powerful, label younger people as potentially criminal, or suspicious, and tend to stop and arrest them more often. This police attention may be the reason why young people appear more in the statistics, suggesting that the statistics may tell us more about police behaviour and prejudices than about juvenile delinquency.

Similarly, the mass media over-focus on young people by creating moral panics (see pp 48–49) around their activities, according to sociologists such as Stan Cohen, Jock Young and Sarah Thornton. Their activities are more likely to be reported in a sensationalist, exaggerated and stereotyped fashion, as folk devils, presented as a threat to society. Such moral panics put pressure on politicians to bring in new laws to control young people, which usually further criminalize them. Pressure is also put on the police and courts to crack down on them in terms of, for example, arrests and prison sentences. These factors result in more young people being arrested, convicted and showing up in the crime statistics. The result of these moral panics may be even more anti-social and delinquent behaviour, as these young people react to what they perceive as being unfair treatment.

Left Realists, John Lea and Jock Young (see pp 26–27), argue that working-class and black juvenile delinquency is caused by:

- Relative deprivation – young working-class and black people may feel economically and socially deprived compared with their middle-class and white peers, in terms of, for example, income, standard of living, access to designer goods, jobs and education.
- Marginalization – young working-class and black people may feel powerless to change their situation using conventional and legitimate means. Moreover, they may feel that those in power are more interested in harassing them through police stop and search than through seeking to improve their economic and social situation. These feelings of powerlessness are likely to lead to frustration and resentment.
- Young people with similar attitudes may unite in the form of subcultures – territorial gangs or other forms of collective criminality through which they express their discontent.

Finally, Right Realist Travis Hirschi (see p 29) notes that the older people get, the less likely they are to commit crime, as they have acquired specific controls, which make them think twice about crime. Hirschi argues that most criminality is the product of a rational decision – criminals weigh up the costs (the chances of being caught and punished) and the benefits (rewards) of crime. The older a person gets, the greater the costs (for example, people form attachments and may have children, they may be committed to jobs, careers and mortgages, or they may have acquired a positive reputation that they don't want to lose), and the more conservative he or she becomes, believing in the rules of society. Young people are less likely to have these controls and are therefore more likely to commit crime.

However, Hirschi's theory has been criticized for suggesting that crime is thought through rationally – postmodern critics suggest that crime is more spontaneous than this. For example, Lyng argues that crime is often committed on the spur of the moment, with no prior thinking, often as a type of gamble, or in a search for excitement.

Examiners' notes

Ensure that you able to illustrate and evaluate moral panic with reference to studies of specific panics such as 'mods' and 'rockers' (Cohen), 'hippie drugtakers' (Young), 'hoodies' (Jack Fawbert) and 'ravers' (Thornton).

Essential notes

Hirschi's notion of controls is an important idea. Regarding youth, he notes that they do not have strong attachments to relationships or careers, and a good reputation might not be as attractive to them as having a bad reputation. They are more likely to be interested in testing authority rather than conforming to the rules.

Examiners' notes

Postmodernist ideas on crime and deviance are becoming increasingly important in explaining and evaluating juvenile delinquency. Be aware of the ideas of Lyng and Katz on crime as an aspect of living on the edge as a source of excitement in lives that are usually denied such opportunity.

Essential notes

Positivist sociologists generally view the research methodology of the BCS as highly scientific because it is a standardized measuring tool in that nearly 47 000 people are exposed to the same set of questions. The BCS is thought to be highly reliable and **objective** and its sample is representative of UK society. It collects quantified data that can easily be organized into graphs and charts for comparison and **correlation**.

Victimization

The British Crime Survey

Victim (or victimization) surveys are an attempt to gain a better understanding of the reality of crime than is provided by the official crime statistics (OCS). The British Crime Survey (BCS), conducted by the Home Office, is a major victim survey that was started in 1983. It is now conducted annually.

The BCS is a face-to-face survey. Originally, during 1983 and 2006, it targeted between 8000 and 11 000 people. However, the 2008 survey conducted 46 983 face-to-face structured interviews with a sample of people aged 16 and over living in private households in England and Wales. Twenty-two trained interviewers used laptop computers to record the responses. Using random sampling (to give every member of the sample an equal chance of being selected), rather than non-random-sampling (whereby every member of the sample population would not have an equal chance of being in the sample), a sample is selected from the Postcode Address File – a database containing all known addresses and postcodes in the UK. The BCS sample is designed to be as nationally representative as possible in order to generalize the results to the country as a whole. The overall response rate in 2007 was 76%, although this was lower in inner-city areas.

The interview schedule, or questionnaire, is composed of pre-coded closed questions with fixed choice responses to make it easy to quantify and turn into statistical data. The interview schedule takes about 48 minutes to complete, and has questions about personal experiences of being a crime victim during the past year. The focus is on property crimes such as vehicle-related thefts and burglary, and violent crimes such as assaults.

The findings of the BCS

Over the years, data collected from the BCS have suggested that:

- Throughout the 1990s, a minority of crimes (one in four) were reported to the police – this suggested that police-recorded crime statistics were the tip of a much larger crime iceberg. However, the latest BCS statistics indicate that the gap between crime reported to the BCS and crimes reported to and recorded by the police is at its most narrow since 1983. This confirms that crime is now falling.
- BCS data confirms that the majority of crimes in 2009 are still property related.
- Violent crime represents around a fifth (21%) of BCS crime, compared to the 19% shown in police statistics. However, half of violent crime involves no injury and since 2007, BCS violent crime has fallen by 12%.
- The risk of becoming a victim of crime has fallen from 24% to 22%, representing nearly one million fewer victims. Overall, only 3% of adults had faced violent crime in the last year.
- BCS data suggests that women worry more about all crimes, except vehicle crime. However, the surveys also show that people who fear

violent crime most (the elderly and women) are least likely to be victims. Conversely, people who fear crime least (young men) are most likely to be victims.

The strengths of the BCS

The BCS is thought to provide a reliable reflection of the actual extent of household and personal crime because it includes crimes not reported to or recorded by the police. Supporters of the BCS claim that these surveys are more valid than the OCS, as they uncover the dark figure of crime – crimes not reported to the police and therefore not recorded. The BCS is also unaffected by changes in police counting rules.

The use of structured interviews offers greater opportunity for reliable data because both questions and responses are standardized and the interviews are piloted in advance.

The limitations of BCS methodology

However, the survey does have some weaknesses:

- It does not cover commercial victimization such as thefts from businesses and shops, and fraud.
- It excludes victimless crimes such as possession of drugs and prostitution.
- It does not currently cover crimes against children, although it will in future years.
- Ellington argues that the samples used by the BCS are not representative of the national population because owner-occupiers and 16- to 24-year-olds are generally over-represented, whereas the unemployed are under-represented.
- The BCS is not really 'British', as it does not cover Scotland and Northern Ireland.
- The BCS relies on victims having objective knowledge of the crimes committed against them but people's memories of traumatic events are often unreliable.
- People may be unaware that they have been victims – especially children or the elderly.
- Marxists point out that the general public are usually unaware that they may have been victims of crimes committed by the economically powerful such as corporate crimes.
- Pilkington notes that the BCS distorts the meaning of the numbers – violent and sexual offences against the person may constitute a relatively small proportion of recorded offences, but these crimes often have a more traumatic effect on victims, compared to property crime.
- Left and Right Realist sociologists argue that the BCS tells us little about the day-to-day experience of living in high crime areas such as the inner city or problem council estates.

Examiners' notes

Interpretivist researchers are generally critical of methods such as structured interviews, as they are inflexible and rarely allow researchers access to qualitative data about people's motives, feelings and fears. The use of pre-coded answers restricts respondents' choices of response to the sociologist's interpretation of the reality. Interpretivists argue that structured interviews are artificial devices that create barriers between researchers and their samples.

☞ This topic continues on the next two pages

Essential notes

Interpretivist sociologists argue that unstructured interviews can produce more validity in terms of the quality of data because they place the interviewee at the centre of the research. Unstructured interviews are not restricted by pre-planned questions and tick boxes. A skilled interviewer is flexible and will allow the interviewee free rein for discussion. Skilful probing usually uncovers motives and interpretations so that the researcher is able to get 'inside the head' of those being researched and to see the social world through their eyes.

Essential notes

Most feminist research into aspects of the family, what goes on in schools and classrooms, health care and female victimization has used interpretivist methodology, particularly unstructured interviews and participant observation. Feminists believe that questionnaires and structured interviews involve researchers imposing their power and interpretations on research subjects in much the same way that men impose their version of social reality on women in patriarchal societies.

Realist victim surveys

An alternative approach to the BCS has been developed by Realist sociologists, who suggest that the BCS has tended to neglect the concentration of crime in the inner city and on deprived council estates.

The Islington Crime Survey (ICS) was conducted out by Left Realist sociologists, John Lea and Jock Young, using sympathetic unstructured interviewing techniques. They asked victims living in inner London about serious crime such as sexual assault, domestic violence and racial attacks and found that a full third of all households had been touched by serious crime in the previous 12 months.

The ICS found that crime shaped people's lives to a considerable degree – a quarter of all people always avoided going out after dark because of fear of crime and 28% felt unsafe in their own homes. Women experienced a curfew on their activities – over half the women never went out after dark because of their fear of crime. Lucia Zedner noted that this fear was both realistic in the context of this urban area and rational when the extent of unreported rape is taken into account.

Other Realist surveys found that fear of crime is highest among the poor, which reflects the fact that they are most at risk from crime. The Merseyside Crime Survey, for example, carried out by R. Kinsey in 1984, found that in terms of quantity and impact of crime, the poor suffer more than the wealthy from the effects of crime.

Feminist victim surveys

Feminist victim surveys tend to produce qualitative data on female victims of male crimes, most notably domestic violence and sexual attacks in which the main perpetrators are male.

Feminists are critical of the structured interview method used by the BCS. They note that in structured interviews the researcher takes an active role when asking questions. However, the interviewee takes a passive role as a mere object of study, with no role in deciding the subject or direction of the interview. Feminists argue that this mirrors the gender divisions and hierarchies of patriarchal society.

Hilary Graham (1983) claims that questionnaires and structured interviews give a distorted and invalid picture of women's experience. They impose the researcher's categories on women and make it difficult for them to express their experiences. Graham argues that sociologists should use methods that allow the researcher to understand women's experiences and viewpoints such as unstructured interviews or observation. A number of feminist victim surveys have therefore aimed to give voice to women's experiences of crime.

Key study

Dobash and Dobash: First victim survey on domestic violence

The first victim survey on domestic violence was conducted by the husband and wife team, Rebecca and Russell Dobash, in Scotland in 1980. Their two female researchers conducted 109 unstructured interviews with women who had experience of such violence – 42 of the women were living or had been living in a women's refuge.

Dobash and Dobash found that 23% of the sample had experienced violence before their marriage but believed it would cease once they were married. The other 77% had not experienced violence, and when they identified anger in men, they saw it as an indicator of how serious the man was about them, rather than as a sign of the violence to come. The first violent episode usually consisted of a single blow with little physical injury. It was often preceded by an argument, usually about the husband's possessiveness and his ideas about his wife's responsibility to him. This was usually followed by shock, shame and guilt, from both parties. The husband begged for forgiveness and promised it would not happen again, while the wife often attempted to understand the action in terms of her own behaviour – that perhaps she had brought it upon herself. Few women responded with physical force.

Dobash and Dobash found that such violence became 'routine' and 'normal'. They found that men felt they had the right to punish or 'discipline' their wives for being 'bad' wives or mothers. Women, too, expected domestic violence to be a 'normal' part of their marriage, and consequently rarely complained about it or sought medical attention.

Examiners' notes

The debate about victim surveys is essentially a debate about methodology. The BCS is focused on achieving quantitative data, whereas Realist and feminist surveys aim to achieve empathetic understanding, or **verstehen**, and consequently qualitative data.

- Sandra Walklate's victim surveys, based on unstructured interviews, found that many female victims of domestic violence are unable to leave their partners because of the gendered power relationships that shape and govern women's lives:
  - They are less likely to have economic resources for potential independence.
  - They have nowhere else to go (the number of women's refuges in the UK is in decline).
  - They often blame themselves.
  - Threats of further violence and losing their children undermine their confidence.
- Linda Kelly's research into 'survivors' of domestic violence found that many women were undermined by verbal abuse as well as physical violence.
- Feminist researchers, Jalna Hanmer and Sheila Saunders, conducted a series of unstructured interviews with women living in one randomly selected street in Leeds during the 1980s, using sympathetic and well-trained female interviewers. They found that 20% of these women had been sexually assaulted but had not reported the crime.

The mass media and crime

Agents of social control

Certain groups and institutions play a role in controlling the behaviour of members of society. While agents of socialization may provide the 'carrot' by encouraging certain actions, agents of social control represent the 'stick' that brings people into line if they display deviant behaviour. The agents of social control we focus on here are the police, the courts and the mass media.

The police and the courts

The role of the police and the courts in the social construction of crime and deviance is covered on pp 10–11.

Moral panics

Moral panic theory originates in interactionist theory. A moral panic refers to intense public concern or anxiety about a social problem or group which has been focused on by the mass media such as tabloid newspapers. The moral panic amplifies the problem to make it seem more serious than it is.

> **Key study**
>
> **Stan Cohen: Folk devils and moral panics**
>
> Stan Cohen first used the terms 'folk devil' and 'moral panic' in his analysis of the social reaction to various incidents involving 'mods' and 'rockers' at UK coastal resorts in 1964. Moral panics usually go through the following stages:
>
> - The media report an event or group in a negative and stereotypical way, using sensationalist and emotional headlines and language.
> - Follow-up articles engage in the **demonization** of the group and consequently construct the group as folk devils.
> - The media engage in **symbolization**, by focusing on the symbols of the group in terms of appearance and music, which it links with trouble and violence, thus making the group visible to the general public.
> - The media invites people with influence – **moral entrepreneurs** such as politicians, experts and bishops – to condemn the group or behaviour.
> - The media predicts further trouble from the group, which puts pressure on the authorities – politicians, police and courts – to curb and so control the problem. Increased policing and severe judicial punishments may result.
> - A self-fulfilling prophecy develops as the group resists control or acts up to the media. This leads to arrests and a spiral of further negative reporting.
>
> Moral panic theorists such as Cohen, and Jock Young, note that moral panics often result in deviancy amplification – the media reaction increases the problem they initially set out to condemn. What was initially a fantasy problem becomes a very real problem.

Why moral panics occur

There are a number of explanations as to why moral panics occur:

1. Moral panics seem to arise most often when society is undergoing a 'moral crisis' – linked to major social change. Cohen suggested that the emergence of youth cultures in the 1950s and 1960s was seen by the older generation as undermining traditional **authority**.

2. Marxists such as Stuart Hall have argued that moral panics are used by the capitalist state to divert attention a way from inequalities. Hall claims that a moral panic about mugging in the 1970s, allegedly carried out by black youths, served the ideological purpose of turning the white working class against the black working class (see p 36). However, there is no empirical evidence of collusion between the ruling class, the police and the media to deliberately create moral panics.

3. Left Realists argue that moral panic theorists often deny the reality of the subject matter of moral panics and portray them as fantasies made up by journalists. Young and Lea note that portraying such crime as a fantasy product of the mass media is naïve because such crime has real negative outcomes for people living in inner-city areas.

John Muncie notes that, like labelling theory, moral panic theory has drawn our attention to the role and power of the media in defining normal and deviant behaviour and has revealed how labelled groups react to media demonization.

Angela McRobbie and Sarah Thornton argue that the concept of moral panic is now outdated in this era of new sophisticated media technology and 24-hour rolling news. Most events are no longer reported for long enough to sustain the interest that traditional moral panics generated in the past.

Examiners' notes

These are strengths of the moral panic theory, but you need to balance your response to any exam question on moral panics, so you will also need to identify weaknesses. For example, see the points raised by McRobbie and Thornton on this page. Also think about the views Marxists and functionalists might have on this theory.

Key study

Jack Fawbert on 'hoodies'

Jack Fawbert has analysed the media coverage of 'hoodies', particularly the events surrounding the banning of hoodies at the Bluewater Shopping Centre in 2005.

Fawbert concludes that the media coverage fulfilled all the criteria of a moral panic in that it included sensationalized and exaggerated headlines and reporting, which demanded that youths wearing hooded tops should be punished severely.

Control and prevention of crime

Strategies for the prevention and control of crime have generally come from two broad sociological sources – Right Realism and Left Realism. Both theories are concerned with explaining and preventing those crimes that negatively impact upon the daily lives of ordinary people. However, their focus is often quite different, as described below.

Right Realists	Emphasize the individual. They note that people choose to commit crime because the benefits outweigh the costs. So society needs to look at ways to increase the costs of crime.
Left Realists	Focus on the organization of society, and especially the inequality, disadvantage and poverty that result from this and which create the environment in which crime might be the norm.

Table 11
The focus of Right Realists and of Left Realists

Situational crime prevention

Situational crime prevention (SCP) refers to Right Realist measures aimed at reducing opportunities for crime. It focuses on encouraging potential victims to 'design out' crime by making themselves 'harder targets' by investing in more security and surveillance. The aim is to increase the risk of the criminal being caught and/or deterring criminality by reducing the opportunity for crime.

There is some evidence that car manufacturers' investment in satellite technology, disabling devices and computerized locking systems has reduced the level of car theft in the UK. It is also argued that increased surveillance in shops via CCTV or security guards and store detectives increases the likelihood of shoplifters being caught.

Evaluation of situational crime prevention

- Marcus Felson and Ronald V. Clarke argue that SCP strategies displace, rather than reduce, crime. Criminals simply move to where targets are softer. For example, Jan M. Chaiken *et al.* found that a crackdown on subway robberies in New York merely displaced them to the streets above.
- Marxists note that SCP often creates a new type of social inequality – the poor are disproportionately the main victims of crime because the middle class can afford to invest in making themselves harder targets and therefore design crime out of their lives.
- Marxists note that SCP ignores white-collar, corporate and state crimes, which are more costly to society.
- Some sociologists have questioned the Right Realist stress on the rational nature of street crime and have suggested instead that most violent crimes are caused either by the need to feed a drug habit or by too much alcohol.
- Marxists and Left Realists argue that SCP ignores the root causes of crime such as poverty and inequality.

- The use of surveillance may be a problem because camera operators may subscribe to similar stereotypes as would police officers and consequently focus excessively on young males. This labelling may mean that the behaviour of particular groups is more likely to gain the attention of the police and courts.

Environmental crime prevention

Environmental crime prevention (ECP) is an approach that is influenced a great deal by Right Realist, James Q. Wilson. He argues that crime is caused by 'incivilities' or anti-social behaviour such as vandalism, graffiti, drugs being openly pushed and used in public places, dog fouling, littering, swearing out loud and physical harassment of groups such as the elderly. If these behaviours are tolerated and allowed to continue, areas deteriorate, as a sense of 'anything goes' develops. Wilson uses the example of broken windows. If signs of disorder such as a few broken windows are left unrepaired or graffiti is not removed, this encourages further similar deviance. Failure to deal with these problems sends out a clear signal to criminals and deviants that no one cares, encouraging more of the same.

Wilson notes that such disorder is likely to occur if there is little sense of community or neighbourhood, as this means that both formal and informal social controls are usually weak. Members of the community may feel powerless and older members may be afraid to leave their homes. Respectable people may move away and more anti-social elements may replace them. The police may feel that anti-social behaviour is not their responsibility, as they target more serious types of crime.

Wilson notes that public housing estates are more likely to experience social problems such as drugs, graffiti and vandalism and these are more likely to be found around high-rise tower blocks. Wilson argues that these problems arise because residents do not take responsibility for the common entrances, stairwells and lifts. As a result, anti-social elements take over.

Wilson proposes a number of environmental solutions:

- Any sign of environmental decline such as broken windows or graffiti must be tackled immediately, otherwise neighbourhood deterioration will follow.
- All public housing buildings should not exceed three floors and all residents should be encouraged to take responsibility for communal space, so as to protect it from outsiders.
- The police should aggressively tackle all types of crime and disorder and not just react to serious crime. This type of **zero tolerance** was famously adopted in New York to tackle, for example, subway graffiti, fare dodging, drug dealing and begging. Between 1993 and 1996, all types of crime declined dramatically, although critics suggest this had more to do with a decline in the availability of crack cocaine than with 'zero tolerance policing'.

Essential notes

Note that this approach is very similar to and has been influenced by the ecological theory of Clifford R. Shaw and Henry D. McKay. The concept of 'tipping' is relevant here.

Examiners' notes

Any essay question on crime in urban areas, or cities, can refer to Wilson's theory and solutions.

Examiners' notes

Any essay on Realism should include a detailed discussion and evaluation of Realist solutions to crime.

This topic continues on the next two pages

Social and community crime prevention

Left Realists and other critical criminologists such as Marxists argue that both SCP and ECP are doomed to failure because they are treating the symptoms rather than the cause of the social disease of crime. They argue that politicians need to address the economic and social conditions – poverty, unemployment, poor housing, poor education, low pay and racial discrimination – that bring about the risk conditions for crime, particularly among the young and some ethnic minority groups. Left Realists argue that urban crime is a rational response to a lack of legitimate opportunities and the powerlessness that deprived groups feel in terms of improving their situation.

Left Realists argue that economic and social reform programmes need to be administered by governments if crime is to be seriously reduced in inner city areas on sink council estates.

These policies should include:

- educational programmes aimed at improving educational success in inner-city comprehensives and reducing both exclusion and the number of 16-year-olds leaving school with no qualifications
- minimum pay legislation to ensure that people are paid a fair wage so that they are not tempted to become welfare-dependent
- a reduction in wealth and income inequalities, perhaps through taxation
- economic investment in poorer urban communities is required in order to create jobs.

Generally, Left Realists argue that there should be a more coordinated attempt to improve people's economic and social opportunities. If people truly feel that the UK is meritocratic, they may be less likely to experience relative deprivation and powerlessness, and therefore, the humiliation of poverty and resulting resentment that fuels most crime.

However, these ideas have been criticized as being soft on crime and criminals, as they imply that crime is the fault of society, rather than individual choice. Also, Left Realists fail to explain why most people living in poverty do not commit crime. Right Realists argue that Left Realists make excuses for criminals, and that tighter controls, more effective socialization of children and more severe punishment are the means by which society should reduce crime.

Retributive and restorative justice
Retributive justice

Retributive justice refers to the punishment fitting the crime. Right Realists argue that criminals should be punished by being excluded from society – by being incarcerated in prison or being electronically tagged. The emphasis is also on deterring people from committing crime. Many right-wing politicians also support the return of capital punishment.

David Garland notes that this approach, although still popular, is increasingly undermined by the fact that more than 60% of those sent to prison re-offend. Interactionist sociologist, John Braithwaite, is critical of this approach, which he calls **disintegrative shaming**, as it involves stigmatizing the individual. Studies of ex-prisoners document the difficulties of reintegrating into society because of the power of the 'criminal' label. This master status stereotypes the convicted criminal as untrustworthy and evil, which makes it difficult for other law-abiding members of society to accept ex-prisoners as normal members of society. Braithwaite argues that the social rejection and negative labelling is what causes re-offending.

There are other problems with the concept of retributive justice. It does not consider that crime might be caused by poverty rather than immorality or evil. Some punishments may be seen as badges of honour by criminals - there is some evidence that ASBOs, which have now been discontinued by the Coalition government, have had this effect. Finally, retributive justice neglects corporate crime.

Restorative justice

Restorative justice involves encouraging offenders to take responsibility for their actions. Offenders are expected to repair the harm they have done by apologizing to their victims and giving something back to the community. Lawrence Sherman and Heather Strang studied examples of the use of restorative justice across the UK and found that the general public had misconceptions about restorative justice – they saw it as weak and favouring the offender. However, in contrast, their research discovered that victims of crime generally favoured it because it reduced their fear of crime and their anger towards the offender.

Another aspect of restorative justice is what Braithwaite calls **reintegrative shaming** – labelling the *act* as being deviant rather than the person who committed the act. This avoids labelling the offender negatively (for example, as evil), at the same time creating awareness of the negative impact of his or her action(s) on others, thus encouraging remorse. This remorse makes it easier for society and the victim to distinguish the offender from the actual offence and to forgive and re-admit the wrongdoer into mainstream society. Braithwaite argues that re-offending and crime rates tend to be lower in societies where reintegrative rather than disintegrative shaming is the main way of dealing with offenders.

The culture of control

Garland argues that a new culture of control is appearing. It involves governments identifying particular social groups that may pose a threat to society in terms of crime, and intervening at an early stage in their lives, with social and economic programmes to change the ways these risk groups think and act. Malcolm Feeley and Jonathan Simon identify a more disturbing culture of control – **actuarialism**. This involves identifying and managing unruly groups rather than catching criminals. Agencies of social control work out who is likely to pose the greatest risk of deviance and then act against them. The police patrol working-class and ethnic-minority areas, while private security companies police shopping centres, monitoring those who enter, excluding potential troublemakers – defined as the poor, the young and the homeless.

Essential notes

Real retribution requires equivalence but this is rarely applied to all crimes. It tends to be applied only to very serious crimes such as murder.

Essential notes

Evidence suggests that the general public associates restorative justice with **rehabilitation** and reform, which are seen as favouring the criminal.

Essential notes

Restorative justice attempts to restore the wrong or harm that has been done. It highlights the important role of the victim and the trauma he or she has experienced, and attempts to ensure that the offender feels some remorse and responsibility for the crime.

Examiners' notes

The concept of restorative justice is relevant to essays on victimization.

Essential notes

These ideas support Marxist and interactionist views of crime and control, as powerful individuals who commit corporate crime are rarely targeted as a risk group. However, powerless groups are more likely to be stopped, searched and arrested.

The debate about whether prison works is a debate between those who believe in retribution and punishment and those who believe in the rehabilitation and reform of criminals.

Dealing with offenders – incarceration and rehabilitation

Roger Matthews (1997) notes that theories about whether **incarceration** in prisons is an effective form of social control – if it works or not – can be divided into two broad camps:

1   The Right Realist position suggests that 'prison works' because it deters many potential offenders from crime, while taking as many serious offenders as possible off the streets. In the last 20 years, governments have adopted a more **punitive** approach to crime. As a result, the prison population has risen from about 60 000 in 1997 to 84 000 in 2010.

2   The **liberal** position is that the scale of imprisonment (for example, the UK has more life-sentenced prisoners than the whole of Western Europe combined) has little effect on the crime rate. Liberals argue that rather than reducing crime, prisons act as 'universities of crime' and are an 'expensive way of making bad people worse'. At best, prisons are simply 'warehouses' in which the reasons for offending are rarely addressed and little attempt is made to reform or rehabilitate the offender. Some sociologists suggest that prisons actually help to reinforce patterns of offending, and in some cases, produce more skilled and ingrained criminals.

The view of liberals

Liberals suggest that:

- A substantial section of the prison population should not be in prison, as they are either mentally ill or have a severe drug addiction. It is argued that these offenders need treatment rather than punishment and that the UK prison system lacks the resources and expertise to address and treat these problems.

- Many people are being imprisoned for relatively minor offences for which community sentences may be more suitable. In the past, these offences would not have attracted a custodial sentence. E. Solomon (2006) notes that compared to a decade ago offenders are more likely to be imprisoned than given a community sentence. For example, in 2009 four times as many shoplifters were sent to prison compared with 1999. Matthews suggests that up to 50% of the prison population have committed minor offences for which prison is inappropriate and possibly damaging.

- Sentences are getting longer for those convicted of more serious offences because of the pressure from media moral panics. Solomon notes that, according to the most recent official figures, offenders are being sentenced to harsher prison terms than they were more than a decade ago.

- There is no relationship between **deterrence** in the form of prison and the crime rate – crime has been falling for over a decade, while the numbers appearing before the courts have remained relatively stable. Liberals argue that increases in imprisonment, even for serious violence, do not necessarily result in increases in public

Note that this observation can be used to evaluate the crime statistics, as it questions their reliability.

Liberals are challenging the success of retributive policies, so use these points to question the Right Realist idea that the costs of crime in terms of punishment need to be increased.

safety, as most violent criminals (69%) have killed relatives rather than strangers. Right Realists argue that prison may have some effect on crime levels in terms of incapacitation – by simply taking known criminals off the street. However, Roger Tarling (1993) notes that it would take a 25% increase in the prison population to produce a 1% reduction in crime.

- There are high rates of **recidivism** (repeat offenders), which suggests that prison does not deter. Two-thirds of released prisoners re-offend, as do 71% of juvenile offenders, within two years of release. Prison is not changing the behaviour of repeat offenders.

However, Matthews notes that imprisonment may reduce a particular offender's commitment to crime. Evidence suggests that most people 'grow out' of crime and thus the possibility of imprisonment. If we look at the age of the present prison population, over 40% are in their late teens and early 20s – only 15% are over 40.

Evaluation of the view of liberals

- Liberals argue that society needs to look seriously at alternatives to prison for those who are not seriously violent, especially those who experience mental health and drug-related problems. For example, drug testing and treatment orders, according to independent research, reduce offending by 70% every week that an offender remains on the order. If the government diverted treatment to all those prisoners who are mentally disordered and/or addicted to alcohol or drugs, 90% of inmates would no longer be held in jail.
- Community-based punishment such as reintegrative shaming may be more effective in reducing criminal behaviour, although the mass media and general public remain unconvinced about this. Matthews notes that we do know that a large proportion of those who engage in crime think or believe that they will not get caught – so perhaps the most effective way to reduce crime is not to increase punishment for offences or to imprison more criminals, but to increase the probability that offenders will be caught.

Essential notes

This supports the Right Realist idea that as we get older we acquire controls such as attachment and commitment, which help to turn us away from crime.

Essential notes

The most important aspect of the Right Realist cost-benefit theory (see p 52) is the emphasis on **target hardening**, consequently increasing the chances of the offender being caught, rather than on retribution and punishment.

General tips for the Power and Control exam (G673)

The G673 Power and Control unit is assessed through essay questions. There are four options to choose from: Crime and Deviance, Education, Mass Media and Power and Politics. Each option has three essay questions and you are required to answer two of these in 11/2 hours – 45 minutes per essay. Remember to allocate your time according to the number of marks in each question. You can select both questions from one option or you can choose to answer two essays from two options if you have been taught more than one topic area.

It is important to practise writing essays and to do so under timed conditions. This will help you to see how much you can remember and write in an exam situation. The essay questions start with the instruction 'Outline and assess', which indicates that more than one side of the debate need to be presented. There are 50 marks in total, and 23 of these are awarded for a range and depth of sociological knowledge and understanding. The emphasis of the questions is likely to be on sociological theories, but you can pick up knowledge and understanding marks for concepts, studies, and contemporary examples where appropriate. If the question focuses on a specific theory, such as Marxist or functionalist theories of crime and deviance, you need to recognize differences within perspectives, such as Neo-Marxism or subcultural functionalism. This will help you to get more marks for knowledge and understanding. You also need to ensure that the sociological evidence you present is relevant. One common error on this paper is for students to write at length about the historical background to a debate. For example, a question on current educational policy does not require a history of educational policy from 1870.

Of the 50 marks, 10 are awarded for the skill of interpretation and application. This means that you must show an ability to select appropriate sociological evidence and interpret it to meet the demands of the specific question. For example, a question on whether educational policy reduces inequalities needs to focus on the latter (reducing inequalities) as much as the former (educational policy). Show the examiner why you are including a particular theory or study, by using phrases such as 'This means that …'. Gain more interpretation and application marks by writing an introduction in which you interpret the essay question and set the debate in its theoretical context.

The final assessment objective being assessed is skills of analysis and evaluation. There are 17 marks for this assessment objective so it is important that you are able to explain the significance of the material selected in sufficient depth. Again, there are useful ways of demonstrating to the examiner that you are being analytical with the material you have selected, by using phrases such as 'This supports the view that …' or 'This is a strength because …'. It is important that evaluation is directed at the specific view or theory in the question. A common error that students make is to evaluate only implicitly through juxtaposition of alternative theories. For example, in a question about Marxist theories of crime and deviance, a simple juxtaposed answer would have a section on Marxism, followed by a paragraph on functionalism, one on interactionism and another one on feminism. A more directly evaluative way of answering this question would be to specifically criticize various aspects of the argument, theory or view in the question and then include other theories as a further way of adding evaluation. For example, by starting 'Marxists would disagree with the way that functionalists emphasize …' or 'Interactionists argue that functionalists take no account of …'. This moves away from simple juxtaposition into more direct and developed evaluative points. You can also improve your evaluation marks by making your conclusion evaluative, rather than just a summary of your essay.

G673 Power and Control paper (sample exam questions 1)

01 Outline and assess feminist explanations for the relationship between gender and crime. [**50 marks**]

02 Outline and assess the view that crime and deviance are socially constructed. [**50 marks**]

G673 Power and Control paper (sample exam questions 2)

01 Outline and assess subcultural theories of crime. [**50 marks**]

02 Outline and assess Realist solutions to the problem of crime. [**50 marks**]

Power and Control paper 1 (Crime and Deviance)

Grade A answer

01 Outline and assess feminist explanations for the relationship between gender and crime. **[50 marks]**

It is a good idea to outline the patterns of crime according to gender. To improve on this introduction, the candidate could have outlined or defined feminism as a theory, as it is always recommended that you explain the key terms which appear in the question. This response could also have gained some evaluation marks by questioning how valid the official statistics are.

There is a very clear relationship between gender and crime in terms of official statistics. Men appear six or seven times more likely to offend than women. In self-report studies the figures are closer but men are still in the majority. Even when we look at victims of crime it appears that men are more likely to be victims of crime than women. So what have feminists argued about these patterns?

The feminist Heidensohn believes that the patterns above mean that women have been ignored by most criminology until recently. She accuses criminology of being 'malestream' for a number of reasons. The first is that the majority of offenders are male, so it is easy to study the majority rather than the minority. The second is that the majority of sociologists seem to be male, so their work may reflect a male, and biased, viewpoint. However, this bias increases when you consider that the bulk of sociological research that is published concerns the lives of the exciting, that is, young males. Finally, Heidensohn describes most theories as 'gender blind', as the sociologists do not think about how their theory could be applied to females, ignoring the female viewpoint. However, over recent years feminists have become very influential in criminology and some of their views will now be discussed.

This is a strong paragraph, focusing on feminist explanations as the question asks. There is reference to theorists and concepts (for example, malestream) and there is an evaluative tone – notice how the candidate uses the word 'however' to flag up evaluative points.

Feminist explanations of the low crime rate of women often focus on the way women are socialized and socially controlled within a patriarchal society. Heidensohn argues that women are controlled in three main areas and this control means that they are less likely to commit crimes than men. Firstly, they are controlled in the home where they still take responsibility for housework and child care, so they are at home far more than men. Secondly, they are controlled in public because fear of crime makes them less likely to be out on the streets, especially at night. Finally, women are controlled at work where male bosses may sexually harass them and ignore them when promotion opportunities arise. These points may go some way to explaining the low crime rates of women. However, the female crime rate is rising, so social control may be breaking down. Denscombe's research shows that young women are becoming more confident and so are more likely to get involved in delinquent acts.

There is some depth of knowledge and understanding here of Heidensohn's theory of gender and control. There is some explicit evaluation, although it is underdeveloped.

Again, this is a clear explanation of Carlen's theory and it is good to see it being put into a theoretical context. However, the evaluation is just tacked on at the end and, therefore, lacks in development.

Other feminists ask why certain women do commit crime. Marxist feminist, Carlen, argues that working-class women are controlled by the promise of various rewards, a satisfying and happy home and family life (the 'gender deal') and equal opportunities and rewards at work (the 'class deal'). When these 'deals' do not work out and the women do not reap the rewards of a happy home life and a rewarding work life, then social control breaks down and makes them more likely to offend. Carlen's ideas are based on her own research, so are quite convincing. However, her conclusions may be influenced by her commitment to Marxist and feminist values. ☞

A very important aspect of feminist approaches has been the attention radical feminism, in particular, has paid to women as victims of crime and abuse. Radical feminists focus on the way patriarchy influences people's personal lives. Research by feminists such as Stanko and Dobash and Dobash has revealed huge amounts of domestic violence and abuse. These are often not picked up in official statistics or even the British Crime Survey (BCS) because many women are frightened to report their abuse, don't want to threaten their marriage or may even blame themselves. However, in recent years the police have made great efforts to become more sensitive to domestic violence, often setting up units to deal with this problem and working closely with women's refuges. Perhaps feminist approaches to crime have encouraged this process.

This paragraph offers another feminist viewpoint – that of radical feminists. Again, it includes studies and is theoretically focused. There is evidence of evaluative tone towards the end when discussing recent social changes.

The postmodern feminist, Smart, goes further by actually arguing that the subject of criminology itself needs to be developed so that it meets the needs of women more effectively. She argues for a 'transgressive' criminology that goes beyond the boundaries of traditional criminology, which focuses only on crime. Smart argues that this means that criminology reflects the interests of men. The subject needs to be widened to include all aspects of harassment of women such as men calling out on the street, brushing up against women on public transport and approaching women in an unwanted manner in pubs and clubs.

Again, a different theoretical viewpoint is offered here which is very contemporary, including a study and concepts. However, it is somewhat underdeveloped in the sense that it fails to explain why this is a postmodern feminist standpoint. The explanation of transgressive criminology could equally be interpreted here as radical feminism.

There is no one feminist approach to explain the patterns of gender and crime, as liberal, Marxist, radical and postmodern feminists all look at the issue from slightly different perspectives. However, they share the view that traditional criminology reflects a male bias and that the concerns of women have not been dealt with well. In recent years, however, feminist approaches have been very influential in the way domestic violence is viewed and dealt with by the police and courts. At the same time female crime rates are increasing – perhaps reflecting the changing role of women. Feminists need to turn their attention to explaining these new patterns of crime.

The final paragraph is an explicit conclusion, which embraces some clear evaluation points, which relate to recent social trends. It displays good analytical skills by explaining the common strands of feminist theories, while recognizing the differences. However, the evaluation is not wide-ranging enough. The candidate could have, for example, made more of questioning the validity of the evidence of gender patterns and crime.

This answer displays a very good knowledge and understanding, which is wide-ranging in terms of feminist explanations. Though detailed, it lacks depth in places, which means it is not a level 5 response. There is strong emphasis on sociological explanations, and accurate and detailed knowledge and understanding of concepts and studies. This candidate shows a very good ability to interpret sociological knowledge and apply it to the question. Interpretation of sociological evidence is clear and focused on the question. There is a range of relevant analysis and evaluation, which includes explicit evaluation of theories. However, analysis and evaluation are underdeveloped in parts.
Mark: 19 + 8 + 12 = 39/50

02 Outline and assess the view that crime and deviance are socially constructed. **[50 marks]**

This introduction puts the debate in context and offers a definition of what 'socially constructed' means. There is a hint of theory (classic sociologists) although this could have been developed further.

The view that crime (the breaking of laws) and deviance (not conforming to expected behaviour – norms) are socially constructed suggests that certain social institutions and social groups are able to define what crime and deviance are. A great deal of classic sociology assumed that the definitions of crime and deviance above were straightforward. For example, stealing was an anti-social act that was seen as both criminal and deviant. The act would trigger responses by the forces of social control; the offender would be dealt with and the rest of society would be satisfied that justice had been done. These kinds of views are reflected in the work of classic positivist writers such as Durkheim.

However, this 'absolute' view of crime and deviance was challenged when the interactionist perspective developed in the 1950s and 1960s. Interactionists see social behaviour as being constructed on the basis of the meanings people give to the world around them. Interactionists such as Goffman explained how people develop a sense of 'self' by interpreting the actions of others and then behaving in the ways that make sense to them. From this point of view deviance is one way in which people's actions are interpreted and has no clear definition.

This is a good explanation of interactionism, and well linked to the notion of social construction. This paragraph is very conceptual and includes a study; both factors are used to explain the theory, giving it some depth.

This is another relevant paragraph, which uses a relevant example to explain the idea that crime and deviance are relative.

From this social constructionist point of view, crime and deviance are relative rather than absolute. For example, the act of killing a person is considered 'murder' in many situations and the person committing the act may even be put to death themselves if the culture they are in uses capital punishment. So, another act of killing another person takes place, but this one is officially approved by the courts and the state. So it is not the act of killing another person that is deviant but the way that killing is viewed in a particular society – the meaning that is given to it.

This is a detailed paragraph on interactionism, which is very conceptual with some studies. There is some explicit evaluation and analysis, where the candidate compares interactionist and phenomenological approaches to the social construction debate.

The view that crime and deviance are social constructions is reflected in the interactionist approach known as labelling theory. The founder of labelling theory is Becker. He argued that deviance only exists because people create rules, which then get broken. If someone is seen to break those rules they are defined as deviant. If someone breaks the rules and no one knows then they are not labelled deviant and become a 'secret deviant'. Labelling theorists focus their attention on how individuals and groups become labelled as deviants and the effect that labelling has on them. They actually argue that labelling leads to more deviance. Lemert distinguishes between primary and secondary deviance. Primary deviance is an initial act of deviance that may or may not be labelled. For example, someone may take heroin but the police never find out; alternatively the police may find out and arrest the person. This labelling may involve them going to prison. Then everyone's view of the person may change. Now he or she is seen as a deviant, which will change the meaning they give to themselves. If they internalize the label of 'deviant', they have taken on a self-fulfilling prophecy, which means he or she may actually commit more deviant acts – this is called secondary deviance – deviance created by the process of labelling. In this sense, deviance is created by labelling and then it becomes real. However, phenomenologists, such as Cicourel, argue that deviance is ☞

just a social construction – it is never real. Cicourel's research involved participant observation with the police and he discovered that middle-class delinquents were able to negotiate themselves out of being labelled as criminals.

Labelling theorists focus a lot of attention on the process of labelling. One key institution here is the media. The media can label certain groups as deviant and therefore socially construct deviance. One example of this is the idea of the moral panic. This term was invented by Stan Cohen to describe the way the media sensationalized trouble between the youth groups, the mods and rockers, at holiday resorts in the 1960s. The newspapers exaggerated the trouble and this led to calls for clampdowns and strict sentences for the young people involved. This kind of process is known as deviancy amplification – the media actually make the problem worse. Recent research by Fawbert on 'hoodies' has identified a moral panic about these clothes. Fawbert conducted content analysis on newspapers and found that they labelled everyone wearing a hoodie as a troublemaker. They were even banned from the Bluewater shopping mall.

It is not only the media that socially constructs deviance. Other forces of social control also do. Labelling theorists look critically at the police and official statistics, seeing these also as socially constructed. For example, official statistics show a link between crime and ethnicity but this may be the result of labelling by the police and courts. For example, Reiner found that the police have an informal 'canteen culture', which can lead them to label black people as 'trouble' and police them more strictly than other groups. Statistics on 'stop and search' indicate that this may be happening. The same sort of processes can occur in relation to gender. Some sociologists have identified a 'chivalry factor', which means that the police and courts are likely to be more lenient with women defendants than men because stereotypes about women being more passive and men being more aggressive (normative masculinity) affect the thinking of the police and courts. However, this view has been challenged by some feminists, who argue that women may actually be treated more severely because they are seen as 'doubly deviant' – breaking the rules of both society and of femininity.

Most sociologists accept that crime and deviance are socially constructed in one way or another. Many focus on the link between the state of society and crime, for example. But it is labelling theorists who focus closely on the ways in which crime and deviance are socially constructed. However, in doing this they fail to offer a convincing explanation of why people commit deviant acts in the first place. They also seem to take the side of deviants and believe that they are only deviant because they have been labelled. In fact, as Realist criminologists point out, crime and deviance cause great harm to individuals and society and it is hard to see how the social construction view offers much practical guidance in dealing with these social problems, apart from decriminalizing certain acts and the media reporting more fairly. This view has been influential in policing though, as great efforts have been made (particularly after the MacPherson report) to make the police more aware of the dangers of labelling black people.

Another good paragraph of knowledge and understanding of concepts, theories and studies. There is explicit reference to the social construction concept, which shows interpretation and application skills. There is, however, a missed opportunity here for some explicit evaluation.

This offers a wider range of knowledge by focusing on different ways in which crime and deviance can be socially constructed. It is, once again, conceptually and empirically strong. There is some evaluation at the end of the paragraph, but it is general evaluation, not specifically addressing the view in the question.

This paragraph is very evaluative; the first sentence is evaluative and analytical in tone. It focuses on criticizing the labelling theory, but it does link the criticism to the debate about social construction and offers an alternative theoretical critique. However, this is underdeveloped and Realism could have been further explored. ☞

The answer could have also developed a further range of evaluation points. For example, how would Marxists respond? Or postmodernists? A relevant contemporary example of policy is offered at the end as an example of the strength of labelling theory (which is awarded evaluation marks), but the essay does not quite feel finished. A final thought relating back to the view in the question is recommended.

This answer displays a very good knowledge and understanding, which is wide-ranging in terms of the different theoretical interpretations of the social construction idea. There is depth of understanding of interactionism, although it lacks detail in places (for example, Becker could have been developed further), which means it is not a level 5 response. There is strong emphasis on sociological explanations and accurate and detailed knowledge and understanding of concepts and studies. This candidate shows a very good ability to interpret sociological knowledge and apply it to the question. Sociological evidence is explicit, accurate, and highly focused on and relevant to the question. There is a range of relevant analysis and evaluation, which includes explicit evaluation of theories. However, analysis and evaluation are underdeveloped in parts.

Mark: 20 + 9 + 12 = 41/50
Overall mark for the paper = 80/100 = Grade A

Power and Control paper 2 (Crime and Deviance)

Grade C answer

01 Outline and assess subcultural theories of crime.   **[50 marks]**

The influence of subcultures in causing deviance in society has been researched in order to determine whether an individual's subculture encourages or justifies certain forms of deviance. Being quite functionalist in their focus, these theories focus mainly on the influences of the norms and values within certain groups of working-class males, and whether they are specifically linked to deviance.

There is an explicit attempt to explain what subculture means, although the first sentence repeats the word 'subculture'. There is a vague reference to functionalism but the explanation following it does not adequately define functionalist theories of subcultures.

Cohen's study of the subculture of lower-class males explores whether deviance is a result of their failure to internalize middle-class values, and subsequent use of deviance means to attempt to do so. Very similar to functionalist Merton's strain theory, Cohen claims that the lower-class males' failure to enter a middle-class form of youth subculture results in a case of status frustration and rejection of what is regarded as normal behaviour by the middle class themselves, normally involving partaking in anti-social and generally bad behaviour. However, it is perhaps fair to argue that this behaviour may be more subjective in terms of committing crime for a thrill instead of their actions being linked to their marginalization from another subculture. ☞

A relevant focus on Cohen as a functionalist subculturalist and associated concepts such as status frustration. However, it lacks in interpretation, as it is not clearly focused on subculture. There is some attempt at explicitly evaluating but, again, it lacks clarity and is a little confused.

The influence of Merton's strain theory is even more dominant in Cloward and Ohlin's theory of an illegitimate opportunity structure. They suggest that crime is committed by these subcultures in order to obtain socially agreed goals using the means of a criminal hierarchy within the subculture, advancing as they become more and more deviant. Also, in the face of conflict with another subculture, deviance in the form of violence is often used, or finally if an individual is rejected from a subculture they are considered as a 'double failure' and are likely to turn to abuse of alcohol and drugs.

Subcultural theories have received criticism in their lack of evidence of distinct anti-social values in a subculture. Downes stated that young working-class males were simply excluded from mainstream values, but had not necessarily created their own, which justified crime. Matza argued that the whole of society shares a set of subterranean values, but the crux is when people choose to deviate and how they choose to justify their actions, by denial or condemnation of others. Understandably, it is also suggested primarily by feminists that far too much focus is put on male subcultural theory and deviance. Postmodernist evaluation of subcultural theory suggests that crime is merely seductive, particularly with youths and does not occur as a result of rejection, simply for the purpose of a thrill. Classed as a functionalist-influenced theory, subcultural theory is believed to presume the presence of a value consensus to deviate from in the first place, and fails to explain acts of deviance within the subculture itself. Also, oversights are said to occur over gender, as feminists have noted. ☞

This is evidence of good interpretation in the sense that another relevant study is being discussed. However, it lacks depth of explanation, though it is clear what is meant by the illegitimate opportunity structure.

This paragraph contains four direct points of evaluation, but they are all underdeveloped; it is very list-like and far from being a sustained critique of subcultural theories.

The candidate does well to link back the subcultural theories discussed to sociological theory and the idea of value consensus. There is, however, a missed opportunity to criticize the functionalist links here, by, for example, considering a Marxist critique. The final sentence is somewhat out of place and is a repetition of a previous point.

There is some knowledge and understanding displayed here, which is more than basic. The response is narrow, rather than wide-ranging, with the focus being on functionalist subcultural theories. Marxists and interactionists also offer subcultural explanations and including these would have made the answer more wide-ranging. Relevant evidence is interpreted and applied to the question but, on occasions, this is related to the general topic area rather than the specific question of subcultural theory. There are four direct points of evaluation, which are underdeveloped and list-like rather than sustained.
Mark: 14 + 6 + 11 = 31/50

This is a good attempt at outlining both types of Realism in the introduction. It would have been useful to start by explaining what 'Realist' theories in general are, before differentiating between Left and Right Realism.

This paragraph offers a reasonable explanation of Left Realism with associated theorists, studies and concepts. However, it does lack in clarity; for example, a clearer distinction needs to be made between studies of victims and studies of offenders. In terms of the latter, the explanation is underdeveloped, and the candidate could have offered more depth by discussing relative deprivation and marginalization in more detail.

A nice focus on solutions to crime, but a missed opportunity to discuss some policies such as neighbourhood watch schemes and victim support.

This is explicit criticism of the Left Realist view, although the points made are list-like and underdeveloped.

02 Outline and assess Realist solutions to the problem of crime.
[50 marks]

Realist perspectives on crime in society are a primarily structural theory. Left Realism explores Marxist-influenced ideas, identifying deprivation as a key cause of crime, while Right Realism focuses more on the significance of social control. Both perspectives share the idea of negotiating police priorities and changes in social policy. Both sides of Realist theory focus on changes made in law itself to change the amount of crime that occurs.

Left Realist, Young, used victimization surveys to deduce that the majority of victims are poor, lacking in power and face social problems such as burglary and street crime. According to Runciman, awareness of your own deprivation in comparison to others, and subsequent failures in meeting expectations, could potentially cause revolution and inequality, so this is crucial in order to balance out the social status of crime victims. The significance of subcultural theory is considered in a Left Realist perspective, as marginalization from dominant values causes certain groups to turn to deviance, often poor male youths.

The role of the police is important in Left Realist solutions to crime, suggesting radical reform and improved relationships with local communities. For example, larger quantities of valid information about crime from the public would create more effective law enforcement.

However, it is also argued by Hughes that Left Realism fails to explain the motives behind crimes and that too much reliance is put on subcultural theory. Also, whether the policies and reforms proposed by Left Realists benefit all levels of society could be questioned, as Ruggiero recognizes the negligence of corporate crime at the powerful levels of society. Ignoring the oppression of women is also recognized as a flaw in Realist theory.

Right Realism, an influential approach in crime policy in the UK and USA, emphasizes the importance of social control in preventing crime. Social checking of potentially deviant behaviour from going too far is crucial to ☞

maintaining order. Wilson suggests that the maintenance of order in a society is crucial to the work of the police, more so than law enforcement. Potentially, it also helps to maintain a sense of community and respect, and attention to small-scale crime is crucial in emphasizing what is socially accepted behaviour. Wilson and Herrnstein drew on the concept of socialization of acceptable behaviour from childhood, as essential in whether traits of impulsiveness and disregard for others feature in and explain a person's deviant behaviour. Finally, Etizoni claims that lack of decision-making in the local community has led to loss of interest in community control of local areas. The proposed solution is for the police and community to regain sufficient social control.

Like Left Realism, Right Realism is criticized for not fully exploring the causes of crimes. Jones suggested that focusing on minor offenders could also distract attention from larger-scale crimes and that improvement of order in communities would only cause the deviance to move elsewhere, implying that proposed reform by Realists would not improve society's struggle with crime.

This is a reasonable explanation of Right Realism with some relevant studies and concepts cited. However, it lacks depth and makes the common error of 'throwing everything together'. Each point mentioned could be explained further, using studies and examples. For example, the issue of poor socialization could be linked to the work of Murray. The idea of increased control could be linked to 'rational choice' theory and 'broken windows' theory. Overall – accurate but underdeveloped.

There is some knowledge and understanding displayed here, which is more than basic because of the conceptual understanding and inclusion of some studies. The response is wide-ranging in terms of including a discussion of Left and Right Realism but the explanations lack depth and detail. Relevant evidence is interpreted and applied to the question but, on occasions, this is related to the general topic area rather than the specific question of solutions to crime. There is a missed opportunity to discuss social policy as related to Realism. There is more than basic evaluation, though it is underdeveloped and list-like rather than sustained, and without a conclusion.
Mark: 15 + 6 + 9 = 30
Overall mark for the paper = 61/100 = Grade C

The final paragraph includes explicit evaluation but is underdeveloped and lacking in depth. A useful strategy would have been to give alternative theoretical critiques; for example, Marxist or feminist. There is no overall conclusion, which means opportunities for gaining further evaluation and analysis marks are missed.

Crime and Deviance

This is a basic response. The introductory definition doesn't pinpoint what Left Realism is specifically. There are some relevant concepts associated with Left Realism (marginalization, etc.) but these are not linked to solutions to crime, which is what the question asks for. The latter half of the response does discuss a policy solution, but this is a Right Realist solution. It is also explained in a very basic way. Overall, this paragraph is only partially accurate and basic in tone.

This answer contains more depth of explanation. There is no confusion between Left and Right Realism and this is demonstrated through the selection of appropriate concepts and studies. However, some of this answer is vague; for example, what does it mean by saying that deprivation could cause 'revolution and equality'? And how is marginalization linked to subcultural theory? More crucially, this paragraph doesn't spend enough time on solutions to crime, which is what the focus of this question is. It starts to hint at solutions to crime towards the end when discussing radical reform of the police, but this is lacking in detail.

Improving your grade

The following examples show how you can improve your answers to the following Crime and Deviance question.

01 Outline and assess Realist solutions to the problem of crime.
(The answer below gives one example paragraph from a whole essay, focusing on the Left Realist view.)

Weak answer

Left Realist theories of crime see crime as a real problem which needs to be solved. Realists argue that poor people commit crime because of marginalization, relative deprivation and subculture. These all act together to make working-class people commit lots of crime. There is also broken windows policy which was introduced by Wilson which argued that you can solve crime by focusing on the small things, like broken windows. This will lead to solving bigger problems such as murder.

Better answer

Left Realist Jock Young used victimization surveys to deduce that the majority of victims of crime are poor, lack power, and face social problems such as burglary and street crime. According to Runciman, awareness of your own deprivation in comparison to others, and subsequent failures in meeting expectations could potentially cause revolution and equality, so this is crucial in order to balance out the social status of crime victims. The significance of subcultural theory is considered in a Left Realist perspective, as marginalization from dominant values causes certain groups to turn to deviance, often poor male youths. The role of the police is important in Left Realist solutions to crime, suggesting radical reform and improved relationships with local communities.

Good answer

Left Realists have a broadly socialist perspective on the solutions to the problem of crime. It developed as a response to the New Criminology which, Left Realists argued, offered an over-romanticized view which saw working-class crime as a justified response to their deprived social position. This focused too much on the working class as victims and ignored many harsh aspects of crime. Jock Young, a prominent Left Realist writer, wanted to offer practical policies to try and reduce crime. Young noted that, statistically speaking, crime is a real social problem with young working-class men as the main perpetrators, but also the main victims. In terms of solving crime, Left Realists argue that relative deprivation and marginalization still need to be addressed (which demonstrates their socialist outlook) but on a practical level.

Community cohesion needs to be addressed by encouraging community organizations needed to help in the fight against crime by, for example, establishing community juries, Neighbourhood Watch schemes, closer links with the police and victim support.

This displays a clear, logical and well-focused knowledge and understanding of Realist solutions to the problem of crime. Notice how there is an evaluative tone when discussing how Left Realism developed as a critique of the New Criminology. The principles of Left Realism are clearly explained and, most importantly, there is a clear focus on policies and solutions.

Actuarialism	Term used by Malcolm Feeley and Jonathan Simon to describe how social control is increasingly about the identification and management of unruly groups rather than catching criminals
Agents of social control	Social institutions such as the police, which are set up to control and manage behaviour
Anomie	Term, first used by Émile Durkheim, to describe a breakdown of social expectations and behaviour; later used differently by Merton to explain reactions to situations in which socially approved goals were impossible for the majority of the population to reach by legitimate means
Anti-Social Behaviour Order (ASBO)	Restriction on the behaviour of someone because he or she has engaged in behaviour that has proved a problem to others in the community
Apartheid	System of government based on racial separation
Authority	Power that is accepted as legitimate
Bedroom culture	Term used by Angela McRobbie and Jenny Garber to describe the way in which girls are more likely than boys to socialize with their friends in the home, rather than in streets or other public places
Bourgeoisie	Ruling class in capitalist society
British Crime Survey (BCS)	Annual victimization survey carried out by the Home Office
Canteen culture	A term that refers to the occupational culture developed by the police
Capitalism	Term used originally by Karl Marx to describe industrial society based on private ownership of property and businesses
Chivalry factor	Term used to suggest that the criminal justice system may treat women more leniently than men
Coercion	Force
Collective conscience	*See* 'value consensus'
Conflict theories	Perspectives such as Marxism, which focus on division and inequality in society
Consensus	General agreement
Conspicuous consumption	The idea that identity and status are dependent on material things such as designer labels and jewellery
Corporate crime	Crimes committed by companies against employees or the public
Correlation	A statistical relationship between two or more social events
Coughing	A practice which involves the police persuading criminals to admit to crimes they may not have committed
Crime	Behaviour that breaks the law
Cultural transmission	Values are passed on from one generation to the next
Dark figure	Amount of unknown crime that is never recorded
Decriminalization	Reducing or eliminating criminal penalties for certain acts
Demonization	Representing a particular group as evil

Deterrence	Putting off someone from repeating their action
Deviance	Behaviour that the majority see as different from the accepted norms of society
Deviancy amplification	When the action of the rule enforcers or media in response to deviance brings about an increase in the deviance
Deviant career	The various stages that a person passes through on their way to being seen as, and seeing themselves as, deviant
Differential association	The theory that deviant behaviour is learned from, and justified by, family and friends
Disintegrative shaming	Term used by Braithwaite to describe how retributive justice stigmatizes individuals
Dysfunctional	In functionalist theory, activities or institutions that do not appear to benefit society
Ecology	The relationship between the different elements of an environment
Edgework	Originates from Stephen Lyng; refers to activities of young males, which provide them with thrills derived from the real possibility of physical or emotional harm (e.g. stealing and then racing cars, and drug abuse)
Empirical	Based on primary research
Entrepreneurial concern	Way of making money
Environmental crime prevention (ECP)	Right Realist idea that trivial anti-social acts should be clamped down on, otherwise whole areas will deteriorate as a sense of 'anything goes' develops (*see also* 'zero tolerance')
Ethnographic research	Form of qualitative research, in which the researcher lives among, and describes activities of, a particular group being studied
Focal concerns	Term used by Walter Miller to describe key values
Folk devils	Individuals or groups of people associated with moral panics who are seen as troublemakers by the media
Formal social controls	Laws that set out a society's standards of acceptable behaviour
Gender-role socialization	Learning appropriate gender roles
Globalization	Process whereby national boundaries become less important
Hegemonic	The dominant form of something
Hegemony	The ideas and values of the ruling class that dominate thinking in society
Hyper-masculine	Extreme versions of typical male behaviour
Ideological function	Having the purpose of spreading ideas, values and beliefs
Ideological state apparatus	A term used by the Neo-Marxist writer Louis Althusser for those institutions that he claims exist to control the population through manipulating values (such as the media)
Ideology	Set of ideas and beliefs

Illegitimate opportunity structure	Alternative, illegal ways of life, to which certain groups in society have access
Incarceration	Imprisonment
Incorporation	Way in which capitalism quickly commercializes aspects of youth cultural style, stripping them of their ideological significance so that they become just another consumer item
Individualism	The pursuit of self-interest
Informal social controls	Norms that document what counts as deviant behaviour
Institutional racism	Racism that is built into the normal practices of an organization
Interactionism	Shorthand term for symbolic interactionism
Interpretivist sociologists	Those whose approach to sociology and research emphasizes understanding society by exploring the way people see society, rather than by following traditional scientific analysis
Juvenile delinquency	Crimes committed by young people under 18
Labelling theory	A theory developed from symbolic interactionism, based on the view that deviance is merely a label applied to some people
Left Realist	A development from Marxist criminology, which argues that it is better to work within capitalism to improve people's lives, than to attempt wholesale social change
Liberal	Tolerant
Marginalized	A sociological term referring to those who are pushed to the edge of society in cultural, status or economic terms
Master status	When people are looked at by others solely on the basis of one type of act (good or bad) that they have committed, ignoring all other aspects of that person
Materialistic	Focusing on possessions and wealth
Meritocratic	Based on equality of opportunity
Moral entrepreneurs	People, or groups, who try to create or enforce a rule
Moral panic	Outrage stirred up by the media about a particular group or issue
New Right	Perspective associated with the Conservative governments of Margaret Thatcher, favouring the free market and traditional ways of life
Night-time economy	Refers to the way that a leisure industry has developed at night in certain parts of the inner cities, providing the location for many offences
Objectification of women	Treating women as objects
Objective	Unbiased
Operationalize	To define something in such a way that it can be measured
Participant observation	Research method in which the sociologist joins in with the group they are studying
Paternalistic	Patronizing approach that removes people's freedom to choose

Patriarchal	Benefitting men; male dominated
Positivist	Someone who advocates an approach that supports the belief that the way to gain knowledge is by following the conventional scientific model
Postmodern	A different perspective on contemporary society, which rejects modernism and its attempts to explain the world through overarching theories. Instead, it suggests that there is no single, shared reality and focuses attention on the significance of the media in helping to construct numerous realities
Primary data	Data collected by the sociologist themselves
Primary deviance	The act of breaking a rule
Proletariat	Exploited class in capitalist society, who sell their labour to the bourgeoisie
Punitive	Based on punishment
Qualitative data	Data concerned with feelings, motives and experiences
Quandary	Problem or source of confusion
Rapport	Trusting relationship between researcher and respondent
Recidivism	Repeat offending
Rehabilitation	Helping someone to resume a normal life
Reintegrative shaming	Term used by Braithwaite to describe how restorative justice involves labelling the *act* as deviant rather than the person who committed the act
Relative deprivation	How deprived someone feels in relation to others, or compared with their own expectations
Reliability	Refers to the need for research to be strictly comparable – not a great problem with questionnaires and structured/closed question interviews, but it can pose a real problem in observational research, because of the very specific nature of the groups under study
Representative	A sample is representative if it is an accurate cross-section of the whole population being studied, which allows the researcher to generalize the results for the whole population
Restorative justice	Encouraging offenders to take responsibility for their actions
Retributive justice	The idea that the punishment should fit the crime and society should take strong action against those who break its laws
Right Realism	Perspective on crime that sees crime as an inevitable result of people's selfish, individualistic and greedy nature; associated with Wilson and the idea of '**zero tolerance**'
Secondary data	Data already collected by someone else for their own purposes
Secondary deviance	The response to rule breaking, which usually has greater social consequences than initial rule breaking
Self-fulfilling prophecy	A prediction that makes itself become true
Self-report studies	Studies in which people are asked to write down the crimes they have committed over a certain period

Situational crime prevention (SCP)	An approach to crime that ignores the motivation for offending and instead concentrates on making it more difficult to commit crime
Social construction	In this case, refers to the fact that statistics represent the activities of the people constructing the statistics, rather than some objective reality
Social control	The management of the behaviour of members of a society
Social disorganization	Situation where people feel little sense of community or of responsibility for one another
Social interactions	Contact with other people; people choosing to come together in social groups
Social policy	Has two meanings – can refer to government policy to solve social problems or the academic subject of studying social problems
Social problems	Social behaviours that are damaging to society
Social structures	The way a society is built up
Status frustration	According to Albert Cohen, this occurs when young men feel that they are looked down upon by society
Stereotype	Commonly held but exaggerated and often inaccurate belief
Stigmatized	Labelled in a negative way
Stop and search	Police officers have powers to stop and search those they 'reasonably' think may be about to commit, or have committed, a crime; this power has been used much more against ethnic-minority youth than white youth
Strain	Term used by Robert Merton and other functionalists to describe a lack of balance and adjustment in society
Structuralist theory	Theory based on the idea that society has some 'structure' over and above the interactions of people
Subcultures	Distinctive sets of values that provides an alternative to those of the mainstream culture
Symbolization	Associating the dress, hairstyles and music of a youth culture with trouble and violence
Target hardening	Making it harder to commit crime (e.g. by increased home security)
Tipping	Process whereby an area declines once it begins to develop a bad reputation
'Underclass'	Term used by Charles Murray to describe a distinctive 'class' of people whose lifestyle involves seeking to take what they can from the state and living a life involving petty crime and sexual gratification
Validity	Refers to the problem of ensuring that the questions actually measure what the researcher intends them to measure
Value consensus	General agreement on core beliefs
Value judgements	Judgements based on principles and beliefs
Verstehen	Term first used by Max Weber, to suggest that the role of sociology is to understand, partly by seeing through the eyes of those who are being studied; similar to 'empathy' in English
Victim (or victimization) surveys	Surveys during which people are asked what crimes have happened to them over a particular period

Victimless crime	Law-breaking which takes place with no direct victim
Welfare dependency	Becoming reliant on state benefits
White-collar crime	Middle-class crime
Zero tolerance	Right Realist approach to crime, which argues that the police should aggressively tackle all types of crime and disorder rather than reacting only to serious crime
Zone of transition	Area of a city with a high level of population turnover